The Spiritual Dimension of Childhood

of related interest

Children and Spirituality
Searching for Meaning and Connectedness
Brendan Hyde
ISBN 978 1 84310 589 3

The Spirit of the Child
Revised Edition
David Hay with Rebecca Nye
ISBN 978 1 84310 371 4

Spiritual Healing with Children with Special Needs
Bob Woodward
Foreword by Dr Hugh Gayer, The Sheiling School Medical Adviser
ISBN 978 1 84310 545 9

Spirituality, Ethics and Care
Simon Robinson
ISBN 978 1 84310 498 8

The Spiritual Dimension of Childhood

*Kate Adams, Brendan Hyde
and Richard Woolley*

Jessica Kingsley Publishers
London and Philadelphia

First published in 2008
by Jessica Kingsley Publishers
116 Pentonville Road
London N1 9JB, UK
and
400 Market Street, Suite 400
Philadelphia, PA 19106, USA

www.jkp.com

Library of Congress Cataloging in Publication Data
Adams, Kate.
   The spiritual dimension of childhood / Kate Adams, Brendan Hyde, and Richard Woolley.
      p. cm.
   Includes bibliographical references and index.
   ISBN 978-1-84310-602-9 (pb : alk. paper) 1. Children--Religious life. I. Hyde, Brendan.
II. Woolley, Richard. III. Title.
   BL625.5.A33 2008
   204.083--dc22

                                                                        2007044334

British Library Cataloguing in Publication Data
A CIP catalogue record for this book is available from the British Library

ISBN 978 1 84310 602 9

Printed and bound in Great Britain by
Athenaeum Press, Gateshead, Tyne and Wear

Contents

Part I: Children's Voices

Part II: Children's Worlds

Part III: Children's Lives

Acknowledgements

This book was conceived at the Seventh International Conference on Children's Spirituality at the University of Winchester, England, in the summer of 2006. Having worked and reflected together over a series of days, it became apparent that we shared similar passions, experiences and interests, and we made a commitment to engage with the spiritual dimension of childhood in new ways. It has been a fascinating journey, and will continue to be so. We are grateful to all the children, childcare professionals and parents and carers who have contributed to this book. Without their interest, concern and commitment, much of what is included would lack a sense of reality. We are also grateful to those who have acted as mentors and guides over past years and who have inspired our own understanding of children's spirituality. Having worked with children and young people in a wide range of diverse and interesting settings, we believe that the spiritual dimension of childhood provides an essential and yet often neglected aspect of personal growth and development. It provides new and exciting ways of seeing the world and understanding ourselves. This book is dedicated to all the children and colleagues with whom we have been privileged to work.

Acknowledgement is also made to TIDE~Global Learning, a resource centre and network for teachers involved in development education, based in Birmingham, UK, for its contribution to the study visit to South Africa referred to in Chapter 4. The study visit explored how education in the UK can develop citizenship education by learning from the process of democratization in South Africa.

Kate Adams
Brendan Hyde
Richard Woolley

Preface

In recent times, and particularly in Western culture, the spirituality of children has begun to attract much attention. There are many reasons underlying this phenomenon. They include educational concerns for the development of the whole child, building resilience and a sense of well-being among children, endeavours for reclaiming the voice of the child, and a desire to better understand the child's world – a world which is often perceived as being somehow different from the world of adults. Many parents and caregivers, as well as those from various professions who engage with children – teachers, early childhood specialists, counsellors, health professionals and psychologists – now recognize the spiritual dimension of children's lives. They have sought to understand this inherent and fundamental aspect, and, guided by a new and growing body of research, they have explored ways in which the spirituality of children might be affirmed and nurtured. Our aim in this book is to examine some of the key issues and insights into spirituality and its continual expression in children. We do this by examining and drawing on interdisciplinary perspectives. These include studies in the fields of children's spirituality, psychology, religion, anthropology, neuroscience and theories of education. We also draw upon relevant aspects from our own programmes of research to explore these key issues, in an attempt to support those working with children to develop their own perspectives, perceptions and practice. In this book we argue that spirituality is an integral part of children's lives; a part which is often invisible to the adult world and so not always sufficiently valued or nurtured. Such affirmation is possible in a variety of contexts, both in professional environments where children gather, and also in the home. The conclusion encourages adults in those different contexts not only to become more aware of the 'geography' of children's spirituality but also to engage more fully with children's worlds – how children experience their inner worlds, and how the inner and outer worlds interact to shape the spiritual dimension of their lives. In doing so, adults can help children to regain their spiritual voices, which many struggle to find. In writing this book we have attempted, for the most part, to avoid unnecessary jargon, and to utilize a style accessible to readers coming to the text from a wide variety of backgrounds. Each chapter concludes with some recommendations for nurturing the spiritual dimension of children's lives in relation to the particular issues that are discussed. We offer *The Spiritual Dimension of Childhood* as a guide for reflection upon practice, and as a resource for parents and professionals who engage and interact with children in their daily lives.

Introduction

Clearing the Ground: A Geography of Contemporary Spirituality

Spirituality is difficult to describe. It is an elusive and even controversial term which has come to mean different things to different people. For example, spirituality has been described as pertaining to interior life, religious experience, the search for meaning and purpose, expressions of relatedness, transcendence, immanence, ultimate values, integrity, identity, a connection to something greater, and awareness. In some instances there are hidden agendas behind these various meanings. As well, in Western countries, spirituality has come to be associated with the New Age movement, and this has led to spirituality being regarded with suspicion by many people. So, where does this leave us? Is it possible to describe what is meant by spirituality? Certainly there is a lot of ground to be cleared if we are to chart a path through these many terms and agendas.

In this introduction we draw on pertinent scholarly and academic literature to discuss and describe spirituality from a number of different perspectives, including religious, psychological and neurophysiological. We also draw insight from the wisdom traditions, mystics and transpersonal psychology to arrive at a series of descriptions which shed some light upon what is meant by spirituality, and which are broad enough to be applied to a multi-disciplinary approach to this phenomenon in relation to children and young people.

Spirituality and religion

The first thing to make clear is that spirituality is not the same as religion. Although it is true to say that the two share a history, and that there may be a relationship between them, spirituality is not a synonym for religion. Until quite recently, people would have used the word 'spirituality' principally with religious connotations. Australian scholar Graham Rossiter notes that in

Western culture, spirituality has largely been understood in relation to Christian religious practice. If a person was to speak about Catholic spirituality, for example, they would be referring to the spiritual life of religious orders, or to the devotions, prayers and practices of those who called themselves Roman Catholic (Rossiter 2005). In fact, spirituality was so connected with religion that both O'Murchu (1997) and Tacey (2000) have pointed out that, to a large extent, religion has claimed ownership of spirituality. It has sought to control it, and it has argued that it is impossible for spirituality to exist outside of the religious context. In such a view, it is inconceivable that spiritual feelings or values could arise outside of the formal system of beliefs. We argue that such a view is erroneous. Yet it held sway until quite recent times.

However, in spite of religion's efforts to control and contain it, many people today are searching for and giving expression to their spirituality outside of formal systems of values and beliefs. Evidence of this lies in the large numbers of people who visit the 'self-help' and 'New Age' sections in most of the major bookshops in Western countries. People of all ages peruse the vast array of titles found in these sections. When asked, many (particularly the young) would indicate that although they do not consider themselves to be religious, they do perceive themselves as spiritual. Leaving aside for a moment the potential relativistic undertones of such a declaration, this serves nonetheless to indicate that people are searching for a sense of life's meaning and purpose, for a sense of something greater outside of the world's religious traditions, and they are doing so quite unapologetically. Disillusioned, as the research suggests many are, by the Church's apparent failure to nurture their inner lives, people search elsewhere for that which provides them with a sense of wholeness.

In the light of this trend, contemporary perspectives maintain that it is possible for spirituality to exist and to be given expression outside of any religious tradition. In fact, various academic disciplines argue it to be erroneous to describe spirituality as being the exclusive property of any one particular religious tradition, and that there is, in fact, a clear distinction between spirituality and religion (see for example Erricker 2001; Scott 2006; Tacey 2003).

This line of thought was first proposed by the Harvard psychologist William James during the Gifford Lectures which he delivered at the University of Edinburgh in Scotland during the academic year of 1901–2. In front of a conservative and sometimes hostile audience consisting largely of members and clergy from the Christian Protestant traditions, James proceeded to argue that it was the psychological experience of the individual – their inner spiritual experience – that was in fact the primordial religious experience. In other words, he declared spirituality to precede religion. Therefore, religion becomes, at best, the secondary phenomenon – a response to the spiritual experience of an individual or perhaps a community. Given the particular sensitivities of his audience, James' pronouncement was not necessarily as tactful as it might have been. It is not difficult to see how such a statement may have outraged the religious and theological community of his day, who would have found it difficult to accept the proposition that an individual's inner experience could possibly be more primary than organized religion. Indeed, this proposition continues to cause discussion within religious groups in the present day.

Since the time of William James, others have argued similarly that religion and spirituality are in fact separate entities, and that spirituality precedes religion, and, in some instances, may give rise to religion (see for example Hay and Nye 2006; Scott 2006). In drawing upon the science of palaeontology, Irish scholar and social psychologist Diramuid O'Murchu makes the point that the spiritual history of the human species predates the rise of the formal religious structures by at least 65,000 years (and this is a conservative estimate!). The organized structures and rituals that encompass the systems of Hinduism, Buddhism, Judaism, Christianity, Islam and Sikhism emerged and have been in existence for as little as 4500 years (O'Murchu 1997). Spirituality, therefore, is much more ancient and more primal than religion.

However, it is important to note that although religion and spirituality are not one and the same, a person's spirituality may find expression through an organized religious system of beliefs. For instance, Australian scholar David Ranson suggests that religious traditions may provide the context and shared value system needed to provide depth and to give voice to an individual's spirituality. According to Ranson (2002) spirituality comprises an arrangement of interrelated activities within two foundational moments – the 'spiritual', whereby a person attends to and inquires into her or his own experiences, and the 'religious', whereby a person interprets and acts upon spiritual experience, placing it into the social and communal reality, that is, into a system of shared beliefs and values – religion.

Nonetheless, Ranson's concept is problematic because it seems to suggest that a person's spirituality remains incomplete unless it proceeds to the activities of interpreting and acting within an organized system of beliefs. Ranson is not alone in such thinking. British scholars such as Andrew Wright and Adrian Thatcher also hold similar views. Thatcher (1996, 1999) argues that to speak of spirituality outside of religion is meaningless, because it requires a theology for its articulation. However, others have pointed out the exclusivity of such claims. For instance, Meehan (2002) argues that these types of claims fail to recognize that there are many people in Western culture who are not associated with any religious tradition, and yet would describe themselves as being spiritual. One cannot dismiss their spirituality on the grounds that they are not religious or that they do not have a theology to articulate it.

So, while a person may draw upon religion to give expression to their spirituality, spirituality and religion are not one and the same. Spirituality is much broader, and more primal. It precedes any type of religion expression, and, for increasing numbers of people, spirituality will not include formal religion. The fact that so many people claim to be spiritual, but not religious, or speak about the need to nurture their spirit as opposed to nurturing their faith, suggests that spirituality may be a feature which belongs to all people irrespective of whether they are affiliated with a religious tradition, or whether they express an explicit belief in God. In other words, it is possible to consider spirituality as a natural human predisposition, or an innate quality.

Spirituality as a natural human predisposition

There are compelling arguments suggesting, then, that spirituality is in fact an ontological reality – something that belongs to every human being. O'Murchu (1997) argues that spirituality is a dynamic quality which all people are born with, and which continually seeks expression throughout a person's life. Similarly, American psychologist Tobin Hart (2003) finds it preferable to think of ourselves as spiritual beings who have human experiences, rather than human being beings who occasionally have spiritual experiences. Canadian chaplain and scholar Elaine Champagne (2001) argues that the human cannot be separated from the spiritual. In other words, people embody their spirituality.

As a natural quality of it means to be human, the research literature suggests that spirituality is understood to be holistic in nature (see for example Bosacki 2001; Erricker et al. 1997; Tacey 2003). British researchers David Hay and Rebecca Nye have stated that spirituality involves a deep sense of the whole – one's relationship with self and with everything that is other than self (Hay and Nye 2006). Similarly, Moffett (1994) has expounded on the holistic nature of spirituality. To be spiritual, for Moffett, is to perceive a sense of unity, or oneness, with everything, and to act on this perception.

As an ontological predisposition, spirituality has come to be understood in terms of connectedness and relationality. Much of the scholarly literature refers to spirituality in this way (see for example Elton-Chalcraft 2002; Fisher 1999; Tacey 2000). In their seminal work, Hay and Nye (2006) describe spirituality as 'relational consciousness'. It is relational because it involves a person's sense of connectedness or their relationship with self, with other people, with the world (or environment or even cosmos), and for many, with a transcendent dimension, often named as God. It is consciousness, because it also involves awareness on the part of the individual of these particular relationships, although people may not (and usually do not) use these types of words to express this understanding. It involves a reflective perceptiveness, a type of meta-cognitive process which adds value to people's ordinary and everyday perspectives. Because it is a natural predisposition, all people are capable of relational consciousness, although, as discussed a little later in this introduction, it can be repressed or denied.

Spirituality, as the literature suggests, belongs, then, to each person's being. It is a fundamental quality of what it may mean to be human. But is there any scientific research or evidence which could support such a claim? The answer is 'yes'. Although some have argued that studies which purport to claim a biological or evolutionary basis for spirituality are contentious, such investigations do, at the very least, draw on the scientific tradition of objectivity and method to indicate the possibility that spirituality is underpinned by scientific explanation. In the following section of this introduction, we briefly discuss some areas of this research.

A biological and neurophysiological basis for spirituality

It was the British zoologist and Darwinist Alister Hardy who first proposed that religious experience, or spirituality, as it would be more commonly termed today, has evolved through the process of natural selection because it has survival value for the individual. The essence of Hardy's (1966) thesis is that the capacity for spirituality is potentially present in all human beings because it has a positive function in enabling people to survive in their natural environments. According to Hardy, then, spirituality is an attribute that has been favoured by the process of natural selection. Hardy's hypothesis has since been supported through scientific investigation, in particular, research which has explored the notions of domain specificity and brain physiology.

Domain specificity
During the 1980s and 1990s a school of thought began to emerge in psychological circles suggesting that the human species could no longer be understood as being endowed with a general set of abilities that could be brought to bear on any cognitive task. Instead, the view was formed that different cognitive abilities are specialized to manage specific types of

information. In other words, much of human cognition might be termed 'domain-specific'. Such a notion had previously been alluded to by Jerry Fodor with his notion of the modularity of the mind (Fodor 1983), and has since been developed by other scholars in the field (for example, Cary and Spelke 1994; Cosmides and Tooby 1994; Sperber 1994). Hirschfeld and Gelman (1994) argue that the mind is not an all-purpose problem-solving machine, but rather a collection of independent sub-systems, or domains, designed to perform specific tasks. This gave rise to the notion of domain specificity. Hirschfeld and Gelman describe a domain as consisting of a body of knowledge that identifies and interprets a categorization of phenomena which are assumed to share certain properties. A domain functions as a stable response to a set of recurring and sometimes complex problems faced by an individual. Such a response may involve perceptual, encoding, retrieval and inferential processes dedicated to that solution.

From this, it follows, it is possible that such an independent body of knowledge – a domain – exists in the composition of human mind that specifically relates to the spiritual. For example, Boyer (1994) has argued in favour of a domain that interprets the class of phenomena described as 'religious ideas', which may function as a means by which an individual addresses and responds to issues pertaining to religion.

Another perspective in relation to this comes from American psychologist Robert Emmons. Although he does not explicitly use the term domain specificity, Emmons (1999, 2000) discusses the notion of an 'expert knowledge base'. This he describes as a collection of information within a given substantive realm that facilitates the process of adaptation to an environment. According to Emmons, spirituality does qualify as an expert knowledge base, consisting of its own set of competencies which may be understood to facilitate the process of adaptation to an environment.

Association areas of the mind

The concept of the evolution of a domain, or expert knowledge base, specifically concerned with the spiritual is further supported by recent neurophysiological studies that have sought to identify those aspects of the human brain that might be involved in religious or spiritual ideas and perspectives. We discuss this in detail in Chapter 5 in relation to the idea of spiritual intelligence. However, it is worth noting here that the research of Persinger (1996), Ramachandran and Blakeslee (1998), Zohar and Marshall (2000) and Newberg, d'Aquili and Rause (2001) has made significant contributions in identifying the neural machinery that may become activated in enabling a person to apperceive spiritual experience. In particular, the work of Andrew Newberg and his colleagues, and their notion of association areas of the brain, have made an enormous contribution to this area. Through extensive neurophysiological research, they propose in essence that there are four areas of the human brain which work together in producing the mind's spiritual potential. For example, the orientation association area provides the ability to create a three-dimensional sense of body, and to orient that body spatially. In passive meditation, this area is affected by the attention association area, which acts so as to shield the mind from the intrusion of superfluous information. Effectively, this deprives the orientation area of the information needed to create the spatial context in which the self can be differentiated. As a result, the individual who is meditating experiences no line of distinction between self and the everything other than self. Neurologically, this describes the sense of unity or oneness experienced by those who are experienced and adept in the art of passive meditation, such Buddhist monks. Although some consider this research to be controversial (for example, Fontana 2003), such investigation does at the very least suggest that, from a biological perspective, parts of the human brain may have evolved which effectively render all human beings capable of being spiritual.

Absolute unitary being

In describing the neurophysiology of the human brain, Newberg and his colleagues have further sought to explain why the spiritual experiences of some people are described by those who undergo them as experiences of oneness and unity. Newberg portrays the neurobiology of transcendence as a movement towards absolute unitary being, in which self blends into Other and in which mind and matter become one and the same. Such states of unity have been experienced by the sages and mystics of religious traditions of both Eastern and Western culture, but, as research shows, they can also be experienced to varying degrees by ordinary everyday people, many of whom have no religious affiliations.

As the result of their exploration of different association areas of the brain that may become active in producing the mind's spiritual potential, Newberg and his colleagues have proposed the notion of a 'unitary continuum'. As with any continuum, or range, the unitary continuum has two extreme poles at either end. At one pole of the continuum, a person may interact with the world and with others, but may experience this interaction as something from which she or he is apart, or separate. As that person progresses along the continuum towards the opposite pole, the sense of separateness becomes less distinct. This could lead to individual experiences of sacredness, and experiences of unity or oneness with other, irrespective of whether Other is encountered in the community, the natural world, or perhaps for some as transcendent other. In the state of absolute unitary being, 'self blends into other; mind and matter are one and the same' (p.156). Such a notion is consistent with, and explains in neurophysiological terms, the Buddhist state of *anatta* (literally meaning 'no self'), or the Christian mystical state of experiencing the presence of God as the ground of one's own being.

Social evolutionary perspectives

However, the biological basis of spirituality, and its favoured selection by evolutionary processes, may not on its own be sufficient to explain continual emergence in humankind. Some scholars, such as Fontana (2003) argue that spirituality does not necessarily confer any evolutionary advantage upon the human species. If this is so, then we need to examine and to take into account other factors and perspectives, such as the social and cultural components in the evolution of spirituality.

One important perspective which considers the social constituents of evolution can be drawn from the work of anthropologist William Durham. He offered a systematic account of the relationship between biological and social evolution, a process which has come to be known as co-evolution. In arguing this case, Durham (1991) maintained that social evolution occurs in a way similar to biological evolution through the process of natural selection. While, in biological evolution, hereditary units are known as genes, in social evolution, the cultural units of meaning are known as *memes*. Although such a notion is contested by some (for example, McGrath 2005), memes are said to vary from the most basic units of connotation through to the more complex ideas, beliefs and value systems. The particular variations of memes within a human group or community – 'allomemes' – provide the different possibilities from which selection can be made via the process of social evolution.

As is the case with genetic variation, not all variations of memes have an equal fitness for survival. Durham argues that, whereas natural selection occurs as a type of selection by consequences (organisms that are unfit for survival simply do not survive), cultural selection operates as a selection *according to* consequence. Particular patterns of behaviour are deemed as either helpful or detrimental to survival on the basis of consequences. Social evolution then acts as a guided mechanism of change. It tends to advance human survival and reproduction, and, according to Durham, it does so with significantly greater efficiency than natural selection.

It is possible that such a process may in part explain the continual emergence of spirituality in humankind, particularly as it underpins the altruistic impulse. In other words, altruism could be one example of a meme that has continually been selected via the process of social evolution because it has survival value for the human community, and because it has concordance with the underlying biological predisposition to spirituality. Issues surrounding altruism are addressed in Chapter 6. But is it possible that social evolution could have a negative or even damaging effect on the survival of the human species? The answer is 'yes'. Hay and Nye (2006) note that negative social processes can be imposed from outside of an individual or community. For example, it is possible to coerce others to behave in ways contrary to the mechanism of change promoted by social evolution. There can be instances in which, because of external pressure, there is a voluntary acceptance of memes that are not helpful for survival. This may create an obstruction, where social values that normally promote survival are impeded by factors such as propaganda, brainwashing, or even drug addiction.

So, spirituality which may be biologically selected in humankind can be repressed by socially constructed processes that contradict it in the manner described above. As an example of this, Hay and Nye (2006) identify modern individualist philosophy as a meme that has emerged in opposition to biological evolution because of the destructive nature of the societies it has generated. Such a philosophy has tended to place the individual at the centre and has led to selfishness, egotism and even relativism, where, for an individual, any one particular action, value, or belief is considered as good as any other as long as it suits the individual, regardless of the effect it may have on others. The individual has been placed above the collective, and, according to Hay and Nye, it is displacing the traditional meme of universalist religion (religion in its broadest sense), in which the individual is seen as part of the collective and the needs of the collective take precedence over the individual.

Some insights from the mystic and wisdom traditions, and from transpersonal psychology

The notion of absolute unitary being (Newberg, d'Aquili and Rause 2001) in which self and other become one and the same, begins to raise questions about consciousness: how does a person realize the state of absolute unitary being? How does a person attain such a level of consciousness which perceives no distinction between self and other? To answer these questions, we need to turn to the insights offered by the mystic and wisdom traditions and by transpersonal psychology. However it needs to be made clear that, in doing so, we are not in any way intimating that a person must hold to the religious views and beliefs of these traditions in order to be spiritual. Indeed, these particular wisdom traditions understand spirituality to be an innate feature of all human beings, and the spiritual path to be attainable by all people irrespective of a religious or non-religious stance. As well, much of transpersonal psychology, which does have some valuable insights to offer here, draws upon the wisdom tradition for its own understanding. So, with this short caution having been made, we now explore some pertinent perspectives from these fields.

Christian mystical perspectives

The idea of absolute unitary being sits well with the perspectives that arise from the Christian mystical tradition. For example, in *The Interior Castle*, Teresa of Avila wrote of the soul as being the place where God dwells, and of prayer as the means by which the soul is united to God. Similarly, John of the Cross, in *Stanzas Between the Soul and the Bridegroom (The Whole Canticle)*, speaks of the soul who has glimpsed the ultimate state of perfection, of union with God. Others from this tradition have expressed similar ideas. For instance, St Bonaventure speaks of Jesus Christ as being not only the way of the mystical path, but the one who stands at the ultimate point of that path. Meister Eckhart spoke of the eye with which a person sees God as being the same eye with which God sees that person.

Contemporary Christian mystics have continued to express this understanding of absolute unitary being. Thomas Merton wrote of the discovery of the true self as being an experience of finding God. This involves discovering the 'I' that lies beyond the ego – the 'I' which is to be found in the very depths of one's own being. This 'I' is, according to Merton, one with God, or, in Newberg's term, absolute unitary being. In this process of discovery, Merton argued, one in fact comes to discover the divine presence in others as well, because each person has the 'I' which can be found in their innermost depth (Merton 1956). A similar perspective was advanced by Bede Griffiths. In advancing the Hindu–Christian dialogue, Griffiths (1984) maintained that the search for God entailed a continual effort to discover the hidden presence of God in the depths of the soul. For Griffiths, Christ is at the centre of the self. This provides a point of meeting not only for the individual and God, but for the individual and other people.

Eastern philosophical traditions and perspectives on consciousness

The Eastern philosophical tradition has always understood the spiritual path to involve self and its true nature. In Buddhism, considerable emphasis is placed upon the person being able to see through the illusory and egotistical self, so as to realize one's true nature (Billington 1997). Once a person is able to recognize the illusory nature of the socially constructed self, there comes an awareness that in its place exists an expansive state of being, which is understood to be an integral part of the unified whole, which is ultimate reality. The means by which a person arrives at this state is the practice of meditation. The Buddhist term for this state is *anatta*, which literally means 'no self', for the self ceases to exist as a distinct and separate entity. Self and other blend, becoming one and the same. This state is understood to be one's true nature, and in becoming aware of it, a person might become aware of the true nature of everything else.

In Hindu culture, 'self' with an initial lower case signifies the conditioned and socially constructed self. It refers to the ego. It is this self that a person mistakenly takes to be who she or he really is. In speaking of 'Self' with an initial capital, Hindus refer to a person's own true nature, which is understood to be identified with the Absolute, or, in Hindu terms, the Brahman. There is a Hindu tenet which attempts to capture this reality – Atman and Brahman are one. In essence this means that Atman, the true Self, and Brahman, the Absolute, are one and the same (Christian mystics would refer to this as the 'God within'). Australian scholar Marian de Souza points to the Indian greeting *namaste* as reflecting this reality. In loose translation, *namaste* may be rendered as 'The Divine Presence in me meets the Divine Presence in you. I bow to the Divine Presence in you' (de Souza 2005, p.42).

Insights from these Eastern traditions suggest that it is possible for a person to be able to expand awareness so as to transcend the superficial self – the ego – in order to realize the true Self. For example, the Eastern philosopher, Sri Aurobindo, drew attention to the notion of ascending planes of consciousness from *matter* to *satchitananda*. These planes include the lower levels, such as the material plane, and extend through to the higher planes of Supramental and Divine consciousness. According to Aurobindo, each person is a self-developing soul, evolving towards greater divinity (Marshak and Litfin 2002). When a person reaches the highest level, she or he may be said to have realized the true Self.

The Advaita Vendanta school of Hinduism is a typical example of a discipline which reflects the notion of developmental levels of consciousness. This model has six major levels, each, with the exception of the last, containing several subdivisions. At the highest level, known as the Brahmanic level, consciousness is understood to be aware of reality as a unified field of energy in which the material, the individual and the Absolute, or Brahman, are in essence identical with each other.

Wilber's integral theory of consciousness

Transpersonal psychologist Ken Wilber has made a sustained and authentic attempt to link the notion of developmental levels of consciousness that are recognized in Eastern philosophy with Western science. Beginning with the notion that consciousness involves a number of different waves, lines and states, Wilber (2000) developed an integral theory of consciousness, in which the developmental levels of consciousness are envisaged as a holarchy from matter to life to mind to soul to spirit, arranged along what he terms as the 'great rainbow or spectrum' (p.148) of consciousness. Along this spectrum, Wilber has incorporated many of the major psychological and wisdom traditions – Eastern and Western, as well as ancient and modern. Across this spectrum, the higher levels of consciousness are understood to enfold the preceding levels. Wilber points out that this type of thinking reflects the philosophy of Aurobindo, who envisaged spiritual evolution as conforming to a logic of successive unfolding. The higher, transpersonal levels of consciousness do not simply sit on top of lower levels. As these higher levels unfold, they envelop the lower levels of consciousness. Wilber describes these levels as 'waves' because they are fluid, and overlap lower levels of consciousness in the way that waves appear to do. Wilber portrays these waves as 'concentric spheres of increasing embrace, inclusion, and holistic capacity' (p.147).

However, the fundamental concept of Wilber's theory is the self, or self-system, which acts as a means by which to integrate the different waves of consciousness. According to Wilber, waves of consciousness are, in themselves, devoid of an intrinsic self-sense. One of the primary features of self is its capacity to identify with the basic levels of consciousness and to integrate the various components of the psyche. Wilber envisages self as a centre of gravity, with the various levels, lines and states of consciousness orbiting around the integrating tendency of self.

Wilber's theory enhances the credibility of the existence of different levels of consciousness, and serves to broaden the perspective to include levels other than the three widely referred to in Western psychological literature – conscious, subconscious, and unconscious. Wilber further suggests that an integral theory of consciousness may assist in explaining how self, through integrating higher levels of consciousness with lower levels, might achieve unity with the Absolute, where, in the Buddhist tradition, one attains the state of *anatta*, or 'no self', or where, in the Hindu understanding, Atman and Brahman become one, or, in the Christian mystical tradition, one passes through the centre of the soul to find God.

So, while spirituality is concerned with a sense of connectedness to self, other, the world, and possibly with the transcendent, Christian mystical traditions, Eastern philosophical and transpersonal psychological perspectives suggest that spirituality may also be concerned with a movement to absolute unitary being in which Self and Other become one and the same. While the notion of connectedness implies two objects being in relationship or connected to each other, absolute unitary being implies one (Hyde 2008). For some people, this type of unity can be achieved; for others, their experience of the spiritual may be plotted somewhere else along the unitary continuum, where connectedness rather than unity may be a characterizing feature.

Conclusion

As this introduction has shown, there are quite a number of different perspectives which may help us to understand what is meant by the word 'spirituality'. So, what does all of this mean for you, the reader of this book? Has this brief geography of contemporary spirituality shed any light upon the meaning of this term? While we cannot arrive at a single definition of spirituality, the following points of summary, or points of description, may at least provide us with a way forward.

- Spirituality is not synonymous with religion. Spirituality is the primordial experience of human beings, out of which a religious response or a religious tradition may emerge. Many people today would describe themselves as being spiritual, but not religious. This is a theme you will notice flowing through many of the chapters of this book.

- Spirituality may be considered a natural predisposition of the human person. It is ontological – it belongs to each person's being. It is an attribute that has continually been selected in the process of the evolution of the human species. Neurophysiological research supports this notion. It can also be explained in part by the process of social evolution.

- For many people, spirituality concerns their sense of connectedness and relationality with self, others, the world (or cosmos), and for many it also includes a sense of connectedness and relationality with a transcendent dimension, which many explicitly name as God. One does not have to be an adherent to a particular religious tradition to experience a sense of connectedness to a transcendent dimension. Many people who do not adhere to any particular religious tradition would claim to believe in God, or some kind of life force to which they feel connected.

- For some people, and at different times, spirituality may involve a movement towards absolute unitary being. This may typically occur where a person feels a sense of unity with Self and with everything other than Self. Ordinary and everyday people, including children, may at times experience this sense of unity with their world, albeit momentarily, or for short periods of time (see Hyde 2008).

These points of summary and descriptions are by no means exhaustive. There are others. But those offered above do at least go some way in providing a starting point – a way forward in describing the phenomenon of spirituality.

The following chapters of this book explore key issues and insights into spirituality and its continual expression in children. The book has been divided into three parts. Part I is entitled 'Children's Voices'. The two chapters in this part affirm the natural predisposition of spirituality, and each serves to indicate how this dimension of childhood can be suppressed by socially constructed forces. Chapter 1 explicitly identifies one of these forces as Western society, which can effectively silence the child's spiritual voice. In this chapter we also offer some recommendations to help children regain their spiritual voice. Chapter 2 highlights the importance of identity and a sense of self for the child in searching for and reclaiming a voice. Again, some suggestions are offered for enabling children to search for their sense of self and voice.

Part II is entitled 'Children's Worlds'. In Chapter 3 we explore the many types of experiences which the worlds of children comprise, and which might be termed 'spiritual', and in Chapter 4 we highlight some of the difficult existential questions and issues of life and living which abound in the world of contemporary childhood. These questions relate to issues of meaning and value, and include issues of life, death, healthy relationships, loss and grief. Chapter 5 explores the notion of spiritual intelligence as a means by which to address problems of meaning and value in life. In it we discuss the plausibility of spiritual intelligence, drawing upon the biological and neurophysiological basis suggested in this introduction. We then offer some suggestions for recognizing the validity of spiritual intelligence and for helping children to develop and nurture their spiritual intelligence.

Part III is entitled 'Children's Lives'. In it we discuss elements of the lives of children which impact upon their spirituality, including their worldviews (Chapter 6), the significance of context and how it shapes the spiritual dimension for children (Chapter 7), and spiritual dreams and how children may make meaning from these types of dreams (Chapter 8). At the conclusion of each of these chapters, suggestions are again offered for adults who work and engage with children, in terms of nurturing the spirituality of those in their care.

Having attempted to clear the ground, and having at least provided a way forward in describing the phenomenon of spirituality, we are now in a position to explore some of the key issues and insights which are pertinent to a consideration of the spiritual dimension of childhood, drawing on interdisciplinary perspectives. It is our hope that these will be of support to you, the reader, in whatever capacity you engage with children, be it as a parent or in some professional capacity. It is our hope that the following chapters will assist you in developing your own perspectives, perceptions and practice in relation to the spiritual dimension of childhood.

PART I
Children's Voices

CHAPTER 1

Silenced by Society: Hearing the Child's Voice

People who are fascinated by the spiritual life of children and who are open to their multifaceted and engaging worlds are usually able to retell children's stories with great clarity. Yet in Western societies as a whole, children's spirituality remains a largely hidden phenomenon, mentioned by neither adults nor children in general discourse. This is a somewhat paradoxical situation, given the current rise in importance accorded to hearing the child's voice, which is embedded in legislation on an international scale. In this chapter we explore the circumstances that have arisen which give children a voice about their present lives, their future and their human rights. We also contrast these with the circumstances that appear to have denied many children their spiritual voice. The chapter then moves on to consider how the child's voice can be heard in matters of spirituality in different contexts, outlining the difficulties which both children and adults face – issues which are developed further in later chapters. Ways forward for adults engaging with children are then considered, and we argue that more adults need to respect and hear the spiritual voice of children. In doing so, adults will be empowered to nurture both children's spirituality and their expression of it.

Sharing the spiritual

Many children have rich and varied spiritual lives, and when they choose to share them with adults, these can be moving experiences for the listener. Whilst the variety of spiritual experiences is explored and elaborated upon in Part II, two examples are offered here to illustrate the type of experience which some children have. Tobin Hart (2003) recounts the narrative of Sydney, an 18-month-old child who lived in a Victorian house in the USA. Her parents told how Sydney would regularly stare at a rocking-chair in her bedroom. Although seemingly motionless, Sydney's eyes would move back and forth as if she were watching it rock, and she would point and say, 'Lady!' The occurrence did not seem to cause her fear or distress. One afternoon, a friend was clearing out some photographs from a desk in the house, when a picture fell to the floor. Sydney saw it and pointed, shouting excitedly, 'Lady!' When the family friend asked if it was the lady who Sydney saw in her room, she replied, 'Yupeeee!!' The photograph was of Sydney's great-grandmother, who had lived in the house twenty years before Sydney was born (Hart 2003, p.133).

A second example relates to a dream which made a significant spiritual impact upon David, a ten-year-old boy from a Christian background, living in the UK, who had fallen out with his best friend after an argument. For all children who lose their best friends, the consequences can be potentially devastating, leading to a range of possible emotions including anger, resentment, jealousy, and a sense of betrayal and/or loneliness. David was no exception, and felt particularly saddened and lonely after the argument. That night, he had a dream which resulted not only in reconciliation between himself and his friend, but also brought him closer to God.

> In the dream David was floating up through the clouds and saw a concrete path. On the path he saw a large 'shining' man, whom he believed to be God, and the friend with whom he had had a disagreement. The shining figure floated away, leaving David and his friend together. They shook hands and the dream ended. David explained that he thought that the reason they achieved reconciliation in the dream was because the man had left them alone. This gave them the time 'to think', and the opportunity to resolve their differences 'in quiet instead of making up in crowds, or crowds of children'. Shortly after the dream, the two friends were reunited. (Adams 2003, p.109)

This was a moving story, which we mention again in Chapter 8. These two accounts are indicative of children's spiritual experiences which can make an impact on them in different ways. Although David was uninhibited in his disclosure when he spoke to us, such articulation is not typical in the course of daily life. This may be surprising, given that children in Western societies now enjoy so much freedom of expression and are usually confident in conveying their desires, thoughts and ideas. To explore why David's articulation was not typical, we first need to examine the contexts which have afforded children that expression, before exploring why the spiritual voice has largely been silenced by society.

Legislating for the child's voice

In recent years, the child's voice has been on the political agenda. In 1989, the United Nations Convention on the Rights of the Child (UNCRC) brought the issue to the fore. It gave children the right to participate in decisions which affect them (Article 12), the right to freedom of expression (Article 13) and the right to thought, conscience and religion (Article 14) (Handley 2005). The UNCRC had a strong influence on other countries, with many legislating for the child's right to be heard. For example, in the UK, the Children Act 1989 incorporated this right, which was subsequently reinforced by the Children Act 2004.

That children have this voice may be taken for granted in contemporary Western societies, although historically it is in fact a relatively recent phenomenon. Only one hundred years ago in Britain, for example, children in the Victorian era were to be 'seen and not heard'. Today, children are increasingly heard in both formal and informal contexts. In formal education settings, Wood (2003) argues that pupils' perspectives are essential in improving the quality of effective teaching and learning. Soo Hoo (1993) suggests that traditionally teachers have focused instead on the views of adult experts, neglecting those of the pupils themselves. Education policy in the UK now incorporates the importance of listening to students' opinions in matters of teaching, learning and their overall experience of school (DfES 2005). Further, the government inspection body, the Office for Standards in Education (Ofsted) inspects the extent to which individual schools seek, value and act upon children's views. In other countries, education systems have undergone similar changes. Reva Klein (2003) argues that Denmark has the most radical democratic structure in its schools compared to other European countries. In Denmark, teaching and learning take place in a dialogic culture and two student representatives are elected to sit on a board of governors.

Other formal arenas where children now have a voice include health, family separation and child protection. In matters of parental separation, for example, social workers may seek the children's views on which parent they would like to reside with. In many ways, these legislated rights have influenced social and informal situations. For example, children are increasingly becoming the target of constant advertising enticing them to buy products and become faithful to leading brands. Parents and carers are acutely aware of this, as children clearly articulate their requests for material goods. Hence the child's voice has become a part of mainstream discourse with a range of forums created to ensure that it is heard. Children now have more opportunities to express their views and shape their experiences than ever before in history.

Children's spiritual voices

While the child's voice is becoming stronger in Western society, there is cause for concern that the spiritual voice of children is often not being heard. Evidence for this comes from research which seeks to hear children's voices on matters of spirituality. There is here a deliberate use of the plural: children's spiritual *voices*, rather than the singular form, 'child's voice', used above. This change reflects the growing body of literature which shows that children have a range of ways of expressing spiritual experiences.

Chapter 3 demonstrates the wide variety of types of children's spiritual experience in more detail, embedded in theoretical frameworks, but first we consider how children express them and bring them to our attention. It is, in essence, the way children convey these experiences that determines the levels of awareness that adults have of children's spirituality. Children's communication of their spirituality can take different forms, the most common, of course, being verbal articulation. David's account of his dream, described on p.30, is a pertinent example of how children can verbalize their experience in clear terms. He also expressed his emotions clearly. David was keen to share, and also to answer questions about, his dream and the meaning he assigned it. In Chapter 3 we will hear other stories from a range of international research which further elucidates children's abilities to express their spiritual lives unambiguously (see, for example, Adams 2003, Champagne 2001, Hart 2003, Hay and Nye 2006, Hyde 2008).

At other times, however, children do not necessarily verbalize their experiences and, as Hart (2003) observes, adults need to be aware of them. One such example is a moment of awe and wonder in which a child becomes captivated by a new insight or a natural phenomenon, such as the night sky or the ocean (linking to the theme of ineffability which we consider in the following chapter).

For older children the diary is one means of recording inner thoughts, feelings and insights. The diary is a particularly personal and intimate means of capturing the inner life. Diaries which have been published illustrate the ways in which readers can access the lives of others. Goertz (2006) offers a sensitive analysis of the diary of Anne Frank, the Jewish girl living in Amsterdam, who recorded her life during the Holocaust. Goertz observes how, like all diaries, Anne's served a function 'as a place of refuge, a safe niche in which to construct and explore her various, but carefully hidden selves' (p.255).

Published diaries are, of course, subject to editing and censorship, as was Anne's over the course of different editions. But for the journal keeper who never intends their diary to be a public document (in contrast to a celebrity who writes seeking a lucrative marketing deal), it is an essentially private affair. Not only do diaries serve as a means of inner exploration, but also as a means of expression of voice, albeit not a voice intended for others to hear. Goertz (2006, p.261) describes them as 'silenced or hidden voices'. Her phrase can be applied to children's spiritual voices – voices that are silenced by society, voices that exist but are often deliberately hidden. The diary is a potential means of releasing such voices.

Silenced by society: Losing the child's voice

Why is it, then, that children often feel they do not have a spiritual voice? Wider cultural norms are the key to exploring the answers to this question, and some context for the term 'spiritual' is needed here. When discussing spiritual experiences, there can be an overlap between religious and spiritual experiences. Some religious encounters may also be spiritual, but not necessarily; conversely, some can be spiritual but not religious. There is often no clear boundary, and academics continue to debate the distinction. For example, Castelli and Trevathan (2005) highlight two major arguments in the conceptualisation of spirituality, writing in the context of how spirituality can be taught in education systems. The first argument proposes that spirituality can only be taught in the context of a faith tradition (for example, Thatcher 1999), while a second point of view suggests that spirituality is innate, and so not dependent upon a faith stance. Hay and Nye (2006) are strong proponents of this latter argument and stress that a person can talk about God without being spiritual, and that a person can also be spiritual without talking about God. Of course, religious language is often the type of language adopted when talking about spiritual experiences, but the two can also be separate.

As was highlighted in the introduction, this book assumes that spiritual experiences can be independent of religious ones, while some experiences can be both. For the purposes of this chapter, it is important to consider societies' attitudes towards both religious and spiritual matters, as they are often intertwined. It is generally accepted that many Western industrialized nations have become increasingly secular over the decades, although the definition of secularization is a complex one. As Bruce (1995) observes, when writing of Christianity, involvement with a church can be an expression of belief, but that involvement is not a necessary element; people can hold religious beliefs, but not attend a place of worship.

Further, reliance on statistics to determine the numbers of believers has its difficulties too, which Weller (1997) highlights – partly because of the problems of how to define membership, and of methods of data collection that can be biased, particularly if carried out by a faith community. Debate about the possible decline of religion continues in both academic circles and the public arena: Richard Dawkins (2006) suggests that there is contradiction evident in the USA and UK. Whereas the USA was founded in secularism, it is now 'the most religiose country in Christendom, while England, with an established church headed by its institutional monarch, is among the least' (Dawkins 2006, p.61). The relationship between religion and spirituality in the West is a long and complex one, and readers are referred to Hay and Nye (2006) for a more in-depth exploration.

The beginning of the twenty-first century has seen a rise in the public discussion of religion, in part caused by the high profile worldwide of terrorist attacks which have been directly linked to religion. Yet there remain paradoxes. Despite the open, often heated, debate about religion in the public arena, in daily discourse the topic of religious and/or spiritual experiences remains a taboo subject. Further, despite the significant increase in books published under the heading 'mind, body, spirit' or the umbrella term 'New Age' – a consequence of a searching for something more in increasingly secularized societies – many people who express such beliefs are considered 'strange'.

Hay (1985, p.140) refers to the 'suspicion of the spiritual' and writes of the 'secrecy amounting to a taboo' which surrounds the experience of many people. He describes how those who express religious and spiritual experiences are angered by those who deny their existence. As Scott (2004) and Hay and Nye (2006) describe, there is often a fear that if one divulges spiritual encounters, others will misunderstand, ridicule or dismiss them. In short, there is a cultural taboo in the West surrounding the spiritual – one which often labels people who broach the subject as 'weird'.

Children are very much aware of this societal taboo, quickly realizing what is acceptable to talk about and not talk about in the context of their age and social groups. This is exemplified in various studies, including the work of Daniel Scott, a Canadian academic. Scott (2004) gathered 22 adults' recollections of spiritual experiences encountered in childhood and adolescence. He observed how such accounts were often accompanied by a claim that they had never told the story before: 'Even though the experience was significant and influential in a person's life, the story has remained private' (p.68).

These adults had, when younger, felt unable to share their experiences because of societal taboos, and interviews with contemporary children offer similar findings. For example, a small-scale study of children's dreams about

God revealed that many such dreams, albeit rare, had a strong religious and/or spiritual meaning for the children. Yet, despite their significance, a recurring theme in the interviews was that, for the majority of the eleven interviewed (eight, i.e. 72.7%), the research setting was the first time they had disclosed their dream. This was because they feared disbelief and/or ridicule from other people. Paul, a Christian boy, had previously only felt able to tell his pet cat, whom he described as his 'only real friend' who 'always listened and couldn't ever argue...about anything' (Adams 2001, p.106).

A subsequent larger study, involving 94 interviews with children of Christian, Muslim and secular backgrounds living in the UK, explored dreams which the children believed had a religious connection. This revealed similar findings, with a third explaining that they had not told anyone else of their dream for fear of being ridiculed or dismissed by either children or adults. A ten-year-old girl explained that in the eyes of her peers, it was simply 'uncool' to talk about dreams.

Another aspect which can increase children's silence is one which Hyde (2006, p.165) refers to as 'trivializing'. Writing in an Australian context, Hyde suggests that many children want to express their thoughts and views on issues of meaning and value with others, but instead they make light of their concerns. This trivializing manifests in giggling or chatting, engaging in trivial activity and creating a façade of complacency.

Many children, then, do not feel able to express their spiritual experiences to others. Their voice may be relatively strong in matters of health or education, but it may be weak or even hidden in matters of their inner life. Ultimately, as Scott (2004, p.77) observes, this loss can potentially, at worst, lead them to living 'in silence with a sense of isolation or oddness'. Another significant consequence of children not being able to express this voice is that their spiritual life enters a cycle of secrecy. Children do not open up to adults because they sense the cultural taboos. In turn, their silence makes adults increasingly unaware of children's spiritual life. As adults remain unaware, they rarely initiate conversations. Hence children think that adults are not interested, and so remain silent about their experiences, and the cycle of secrecy perpetuates.

Reclaiming the child's spiritual voice

If many children feel that they cannot express their spiritual voice – even if they can express their voice in other areas of their life – what are the implications for adults? This section explores those implications for adults in different professional settings and in the home, including suggestions for how to read the remainder of this book. Before doing so, however, it is important to acknowledge that some children may not wish to share their spiritual lives with others, even if asked. This desire for privacy is a right, and is one to be respected. Hence it is important never to place a child under pressure to divulge their spiritual experiences, irrespective of the context – whether it be a personal or professional relationship – just as it would be unethical to read another person's diary simply out of curiosity. However, for those children who wish to share this aspect of their inner lives, there are implications for them and for the adults who know them.

For adults, the difficulties of responding appropriately to children's spiritual experiences are numerous. An initial problem lies in adults actually recognizing that children are expressing something spiritual. As this book progresses, an increasing range of spiritual moments and encounters will be brought to you, demonstrating how what one person defines as spiritual, another will not. Some of these accounts will be new to you, others will be familiar. Some will be tender and evocative, others will be unsettling. Whilst some will be overtly spiritual, others will not, but this book will help you to identify them. Once you are able to do this, another important factor is to acknowledge that the experience may be significant to the child, no matter how inconsequential it may appear to you. Again, this theme will be developed further in later chapters. For children, their encounters may be important, meaningful, and may even shape their beliefs and worldviews. It is this element, of the significance to children, which you will need to acknowledge and respect.

One example which epitomizes these points of recognizing spiritual experiences and their importance for the children is the often difficult topic of death. We discuss an example here, since this issue also creates difficulties for the child's voice because adults can be intimidated by hearing it. Many spiritual experiences, for children and adults alike, relate in some way to death, whether it be anticipation of the death of a loved one, images of heaven, or an encounter with someone who has died. Such incidents are regularly reported by children. For example, Hart (2003) describes children's encounters with angels. All adults will at some time be confronted with children's questions about death and what, if anything, lies beyond. Parents and carers will need to face these inevitable questions, whether they relate to the death of a pet or a person; health care professionals are likely to have the issue raised for them; teachers may find a child grieving or pondering such issues in the classroom; and counsellors may at times need to engage with the topic during sessions.

It may be, however, that the difficulty of engaging with issues relating to death lies more with adults than with children. If so, then adults need to be more aware of their need to find their own voice whilst helping children express theirs. This point is exemplified by the tale of Ellen, a teacher, who described a tragedy which befell her primary school.

> There was no easy way for my colleague to tell me that John, one of our ten-year-old pupils, had been killed in a car accident. It had been a terrible tragedy, with no one to blame. As teachers we had to face not only the personal loss but we also had to support the family and the other children in the school. Thankfully the school had never had to deal with a death before – which of course meant that we didn't really know what to do. To be honest, fear and a sense of powerlessness set in amongst most of the staff.

Ellen had always been the pioneer of bringing 'taboo' subjects into the class-room, believing that children had insights beyond what many of her colleagues thought them capable of. Although a young teacher, she sensed her experienced colleagues' fear of dealing with the matter, so she volunteered to lead the way. After she had explained to the other children about John's death, all of the teachers commented on how pragmatically the children had responded. It was not that they weren't shocked, but their responses were very straightforward. 'What has happened to John now he's dead?' 'I know it wasn't the driver's fault, but why did John have to die?' several asked.

A few days later, some began to comment that they had seen John. The children understood that he was no longer physically there. During a maths lesson, Kara suddenly said, 'John was playing at the bottom of the field yester-day. He didn't see me, but I am just happy he is okay.' The encounter had given Kara a sense of ease, reassuring her that John was still alive, albeit in a different form, and there was no sense of alarm or trepidation at seeing what the children might have called a 'ghost'.

Yet the teachers, with the exception of Ellen, continued to have difficulty with knowing how to react to experiences like Kara's. Their story has implica-tions for adults in a variety of contexts. Often children do not necessarily seek an answer when describing an experience which may be considered spiritual, like Kara's. Instead they often seek to be heard.

The framing of a response to a spiritual experience of any kind can some-times be simply to listen and affirm. Affirmation does not mean that you have to verbally affirm the existence of something you do not believe in – for example, an atheist does not have to say that what Kara saw was real, if they do not believe in an afterlife. Instead, it is the role of the adult to acknowledge that the experience was real to the child and potentially meaningful for them. Sometimes all that is needed is a smile or other gesture of empathy or sincerity.

As mentioned above, the child's voice is not always a verbal one in matters of spirituality. Hart (2003) observes the boundless capacity of young children for creativity and imagination. He describes how his youngest child was given a glue gun and spontaneously began to create people, fairies and household objects such as beds, dishes and cloths out of a variety of different materials, including sticks and flowers. For adults, there can be a need for sensitive and quiet observation, which is often unobtrusive, in order to appreciate the spiritual moments of the children around them.

Some recommendations

In this section we offer a list of recommendations for adults, in a variety of contexts, to help children around them regain their spiritual voice.

- Whatever your place of interaction with children, be aware of children's expressions of spirituality. Younger children will not, of course, use this term, or even be aware of its existence, and their expressions can take many forms. Some are more overt than others, as this chapter has shown – from a straightforward verbal account, to simply being lost in their own world. The work of Hart (2003) and Scott (2004) in particular attests to the crucial role played by adults in these instances – adults who need to demonstrate a capacity to listen and to model their experience by telling their own stories. For other children, spiritual experience may take a more seemingly mundane form, and comprise the everyday events of childhood – running, singing, creating, painting, playing a game with a friend, enjoying a juicy orange, rolling in the autumn leaves, reflecting on a dream, or even being captivated by a beautiful sunset. Although most of these experiences seem ordinary and everyday, research attests to the fact that many of them may be (and frequently are) experienced as spiritual by children (see Adams 2003; Champagne 2003; Hay and Nye 2006; Hyde 2008).

- At times, as we show in Chapter 5, children may simply appear to be 'pesting' adults, constantly asking questions, which may in fact be searchings for meanings and value. For adults, alertness is essential and the remainder of this book will help you identify common experiences.

- Once a spiritual experience has been recognized, a sensitive and open-minded approach is essential. It may not be an appropriate time or setting in which to initiate conversation about it – but if it is, then indications of your interest will empower children to feel safe to talk. In professional settings, adults will need to build up an ethos of trust and mutual respect, so that children feel able to say what they wish without fear of being dismissed or ridiculed. In counselling and social work, this is an integral part of the relationships which can be built up over time. In education contexts, Dean (2000) explains how the classroom atmosphere should be unthreatening, so that children are confident enough to take risks. If this ethos also nurtures self-esteem and they are working in a positive climate where their opinions and views are heard, they are more likely to share their perceptions and experiences. A similar theory can be applied to all professional settings where adults interact regularly with the same group of children. For hospital workers who may only see individual children for short lengths of time, it may not be possible to develop long-term ongoing relationships. However, in some cases, all that children seek is an understanding ear to listen, even if they will never see you again. Of course, some people find it easier to confide in someone they will never see again.

- Be aware that for many children, it is difficult to voice their inner life. All too often adults have, albeit unintentionally, shown a lack of interest which has led the child to assume that the adult does not want to know, or will not take their experiences or reflections seriously. For parents and carers, this may be because they were busy trying to get their children ready for school and didn't have the time or focus necessary; for a teacher, it may be that they were under pressure to teach the next part of a lesson or had to deal with a disruption on the other side of the classroom; in a hospital, a nurse may be called away to an emergency with another patient. Sometimes, other factors overtake the quieter, spiritual moments of life, but for adults who are aware of their existence, the likelihood of recognizing and acknowledging them is vastly increased.

- As mentioned above, the child's right to privacy should always be respected. Indeed, over-encouragement and enthusiasm to 'know' on the part of adults can be counter-productive; if children feel that they are constantly expected to 'produce' spiritual experiences and profound reflections upon life, the consequences could be negative, and children may fabricate answers which they think the adults want to hear, or else feel pressured and choose to disengage.

- Always remain aware of the possible consequences of not hearing the child's spiritual voice. Scott (2004) recounts the case of Nora, who, when four or five years old, was able to see auras around her friends. For Nora, seeing these lights was normal, but one day, when she mentioned them to her friends, she realized that they could not see them. She explained, 'I was seeing something they could not see. I never saw lights around people again until I was in my thirties.' Through not hearing children, a 'shutting off' of their spiritual awareness can occur.

- Some issues raised may be unsettling for adults, particularly in the case of experiences related to death and dying, as illustrated above (p.37). Health professionals, including doctors and nurses, are perhaps in a position where they will be more exposed to such questions; children who are hospitalized may be fearful of death, even if they are not suffering from life-threatening illnesses, and may be more conscious of their mortality. But every adult will at some point be faced with children's questions about death, and it is essential that they hear what is being said and asked. Be honest with yourself: is it you who has difficulties talking about death? If so, why? Remember that children will need your emotional support in this area, however difficult you find the topic to discuss.

Conclusion

The increasing prominence of the child's voice has not necessarily spread to spirituality. Reasons for this are numerous and relate largely to Western cultures' attitudes towards the subject, which incorporate a lack of empathy with children and how they experience and perceive the world. Given that children are aware of society's taboos, some actually feel that they cannot share their spiritual life. Yet all they need is an adult whom they can trust, and who will respect what they have to say, in order to regain that lost voice. As a reader of this book you are obviously the type of adult they are looking for, but sadly you are probably in the minority. However, if you can support only one child in their quest for spiritual understanding, then you will have made a difference to that child's life – a difference that could last a lifetime.

CHAPTER 2

Identity: Spirituality, the Self and the Search for One's Voice

In the early twenty-first century our understanding of childhood is most complex and highly developed. Children encounter diverse and sometimes contradictory social roles and situations. Issues of justice and human rights, and issues of child development, nurture and protection are a part of the everyday work of adults in churches, schools and community settings. Actively listening to and engaging with children and young people is fundamental to such work, as is the process of helping them to become involved in the social issues that relate to their personal context. The days when children were to be 'seen and not heard' have passed (if they ever really existed), and the focus, as we have seen in the previous chapter, is now on giving children a voice and empowering them to speak out about their own experiences, situations and aspirations (Woolley 2008). This chapter builds on the sense of the inner voice of the child outlined in Chapter 1 and makes links to theories of child development and social and political aspects of the spiritual dimension of childhood.

Finding oneself: Is child development a useful construct?

To speak of child development in terms of its social, intellectual, physical, spiritual or emotional aspects is to split the child into numerous, seemingly unconnected, facets. Whilst this metaphorical and cultural perspective (Myers 1997) may have its uses, it can undermine the wholeness of the individual and suggest that aspects develop in isolation. It is difficult to consider how a child's development in any one of these areas could progress without impacting upon other aspects. For example, the feelings associated with emotional maturation affect intellectual development; the intellectual ability to understand the rules of a sport impact on the physical development gained by joining in.

Theories of child development are just that – theories. They serve a purpose in helping us to discuss and classify elements of a child's growth. However, they are incomplete frameworks which should not become straightjackets. Westerman (2001) explores the nature of child development, developmental stages and rites of passage in some detail. What is important here is the idea that children do not develop according to rigid timelines or programmes; they do not all mature, grow or learn at the same rate. Hart (2003) notes that developmental theorists typically tell us that children are self-centred and have not developed sufficiently to put themselves in someone else's shoes; they are incapable of real empathy or compassion. 'Indeed, children can be enormously selfish and self-centred, but they can also be deeply empathetic and compassionate' (p.69).

'Development' is not the best term to capture the reality of the journey on which children are travelling (Pridmore and Pridmore 2004). The term has overtones of the developmental stages suggested by Piaget and others. It has connotations of reaching stages or anticipated norms. It can also imply that there is a 'correct' order in which growth or learning will take place, and it can inhibit the expectations that we have for the ways in which children will flourish. The notion of a 'journey' might also have such overtones but, without a specific route map or a prescribed path, it opens up the possibility of a non-linear progression that can be different for each individual. Herein lies the importance of the term 'dimension' in spiritual (and other) development. For it suggests that there is a spiritual element to the development of children, and indeed of all people, without prescriptive stages, processes or targets. A profound lesson learned from implementing the United Nations' Convention on the Rights of the Child (1989) is that at virtually every age from birth onwards children's capacities are greater than previously imagined (UNICEF 2002). This has significant implications for all those involved in childcare settings; each of us needs to avoid pigeon-holing children and young people and limiting their growth through the application of models of development which lower our expectations or cause us to label individuals as 'failing'.

McLaughlin (1996) suggests two approaches to the 'whole' child: comprehensiveness and integration. Comprehensiveness relates to education having a broad, rounded or balanced influence on a wide range of aspects of a child. However, it can lead to the compartmentalization of areas such as the cognitive and the affective, the intellectual and emotional. Such sharp distinctions and dichotomies need to be avoided, as has already been noted. In contrast, a holistic perspective is needed. For even when addressing the intellectual, education is communicating meaning on a range of levels, for example through the 'hidden curriculum', and so the intellectual is not, and must not be, divorced from the emotional. Integration relates to an approach focusing on the whole rather than the fragmented. But what is the nature of such coherence, oneness or unity of self?

Freedom to grow

When working with children and young people it is essential to ensure that opportunities for amazement, awe and wonder are not lost. In the structure of the school curriculum, the hectic activity of the holiday club or the busyness of the medical ward, the inherent curiosity of children, their propensity to ask questions and to be intrigued, their uninhibited fascination with all that is around them, their sense of the being of all creatures, and 'their intercourse with the cosmos' (Newby 1996, p.48) must not be ignored or neglected. Spirituality is about allowing the freedom needed for children's personal growth: 'enabling the creative thinking and relational feeling necessary for the development of morality and a sense of community' (Watson 2003, p.19). However, because schooling is influenced by Western socio-economic values it inhibits such growth: this stifles moral development and undermines the nature of society.

Watson argues that spirituality is about space and attentiveness to the child as a person in need of space to grow and develop. This applies equally to all childcare settings, including the home. Children need to be provided with space in which they can be listened to and where they can explore ideas without too much adult direction. Watson argues that this care will reap rewards in the form of an increased confidence and strength of character in young people, and an increased awareness of their relationship with other people, with the environment, with communities and society, and with the world as a whole.

In a classroom setting, teachers usually require that their pupils are attentive and 'on task'. Indeed, in the UK, when schools are inspected, one of the tell-tale signs of less than satisfactory teaching is the number of children who are not engaged with an activity. Yet where are these children? Where do they go when they drift 'off task' and daydream or lose concentration? Perhaps they inhabit a realm much understood, but not always acknowledged, by their adult counterparts (for which of us does not have occasional 'down time' when we are meant to be engaged in important elements of our own work?). The problem is that schools prefer certainty to mystery (Hart 2003, p.51); they require full attention from their students, and for tasks to be completed within the confines of the lesson being delivered. Whilst we are not arguing here in support of poor teaching, it is important for adults to consider how, in their varied and various encounters with children, they provide the space for thinking, reflecting and imagining.

> Jonathan reflected on the number of times, in his career as a teacher, when he had required a child to complete a piece of fiction writing in a clearly prescribed period of time. Even when tasks were set over a series of lessons, with opportunities for planning, drafting, redrafting, editing and final production, he required consistent and sustained concentration and hard work: 'To be clear, I was engaged in the factory farming approach to teaching. The child had to create an idea, develop it in an imaginative and inventive way and meet prescribed learning objectives. Where in this process was the time and space necessary for dreaming, imagining or fantasizing?'

Jonathan's views challenge us to consider how we create the space for children to find their voices or express originality. As writers, we know the experience of being so absorbed in an idea that we lose all track of time; as readers we know the joy of reading a novel that is so gripping that we cannot put it down; as 'surfers' we know that the myriad connections of the internet can take us to ideas and concepts so fascinating that an evening ebbs away. Yet in a classroom the bell signals the end of a lesson, and before it sounds the teacher must conclude an activity and lead a plenary discussion to consolidate what the children have 'learned'. The brisk structures that define so much of our work with children and young people militate against some important aspects of learning and development and certainly undermine opportunities for them to find their voice, explore creative ideas or dream dreams. Tobin Hart (2003, p.94) suggests that: 'in schools, one right answer, often on a multiple-choice test, determines value, worth, and truth. Schools do not lack answers, they lack depth. Depth is associated more with asking good questions than with having all the answers.' Wisdom is the capacity not so much for problem solving as for *problem finding*. Children have a remarkable capacity for identifying problems that we may overlook or take for granted as adults. The following example serves to elaborate on this need for space to enquire.

> One afternoon Mr Watts announced to his class that they were going to learn about sex. There was a sudden flurry of excitement and embarrassment around the class: 'We're going to learn about the sex life of daffodils,' he continued, causing some consternation amongst the children. The children watched as he drew a daffodil on the chalkboard and labelled the parts; then they copied the diagram. There was no sense of using the flower as a

starting point for questions. Why is it yellow? Why is it that shape? What do the strands inside the flower do? What is that 'dust' that gets on my fingers? What is inside each part? What does it eat or drink? How does it reproduce? How long does it live? Do they all have the same number of petals and leaves? The eager questioning of the children was stifled by the provision of the 'right' answer from the front of the class.

This teacher, in common with so many adults, communicated a way of being human through the way in which he approached life. Spirituality cannot be nurtured where learning is delivered in a detached manner, where the teacher seeks to protect him- or herself from questions or difficult issues and keeps the children at arm's length. The lack of a sense of awe at the ways in which daffodils reproduce and multiply, the lack of excitement about the process of growth and reproduction, the loss of interest in the wonder of creation sustaining itself, all contribute to the stifling of opportunities for children to marvel and learn. If one cannot marvel at the intricacies of the natural world, how can one learn to find one's voice to express concerns about the destruction of the planet, care for its resources, appreciate its beauty or its complexities? This raises several other issues and questions:

- How do we develop participatory methods to engage children so that issues have a *livingness* and a reality to them?

- How do we ensure that learning is not compartmentalized into subject-based elements which detract from the interconnectedness of ideas?

- How do we contextualize our work with children so that it has a global rather than a fragmented dimension?

- How do we create the space for the unexpected question that leads to new learning?

All these questions require us to consider the notion that the whole is greater than all its parts: we need an integrating approach both in our conception of models of child development and in our approaches to supporting that development. These principles apply to the classroom and also extend well beyond it – into any formal and informal situations where children learn from adults.

Scaffolding the awareness of self

Within what Vygotsky called 'the zone of proximal development' (ZPD), people move from the known to the unknown and are nurtured in what they can understand and do with help from a more knowledgeable peer, mentor or teacher. The ZPD is the gap between what a child can do independently and what he or she is able to achieve with the support of another person. Such helping persons provide what Bruner terms 'scaffolding', so that learners can transcend their present understandings or skills (Lefrancois 1999; Myers 1997). They provide interventions that help children to move from their *actual* development towards their *potential* development: they bridge the gap. As children learn, they benefit from this support, encouragement and experience and move towards a position of greater independence. All those involved bring something of value (interests, skills, knowledge, understanding and dreams) to the relationship.

The ZPD may also provide a space in which transcendence can be supported, as the sense of awe experienced by the more experienced partner infects the imagination of the younger one. Nurture in the ZPD is necessary. However, social context may impinge in a restrictive way – if adults reserve spirituality for adulthood or do not scaffold spiritual experiences for children (Nye 1996). As adults we hold a powerful position: we can choose to offer children creative and stimulating opportunities, we can respond in ways which appreciate and accept their ideas, and we can respect the power of their imagination, even when ideas sometimes seem unorthodox. We can choose to scaffold the expression of excitement, awe or imagination, or we can ridicule, criticize or undermine its validity.

Hay and Nye (2006) suggest that the task of nourishing spirituality is one of releasing, not constricting, children's understanding and imagination. Adults can choose to impose socially and historically developed norms, or they can allow children a free space in which to express themselves. We suggest that social pressures include the need to know the right answer and to be able to memorize and repeat it. Whilst we are aware that there is a place for knowing facts (and that building such knowledge is important), nourishing spirituality is about allowing children to question, without feeling the need to provide stock answers; the way to the internalization of learning, appreciation and apprehension is to support questioning and to allow natural fascination. The question 'Why were people made?' raises many issues and ideas in our minds, but to give an answer to a child provides little help. Rather, the response 'Why do you think they were made?' allows the child to progress on their spiritual journey and develop their own worldview: it may be a partial understanding of the world, but so is our own. Indeed, children often have insights that surpass the ideas held by adults, because they have a natural sensitivity that allows them to hear their inner wisdom: 'Listening to intuition means noticing those subtle cues that we often tell children not to pay attention to – a gut feeling, a vague discomfort, a fleeting idea. Sometimes what is heard is remarkably beautiful' (Hart 2003, p.43).

Indeed, Lang, Best and Lichtenberg (1994) suggest that too little attention has been given to the preparation of teachers for the affective dimension of their roles, either because it is assumed that this is implicit to the delivery of the curriculum, or because it is presumed to be unimportant. There may be a focus on the feelings associated with personal and social education, but any spiritual element remains significantly neglected. This point is significant: in some contexts spirituality is a part of the school curriculum, yet often remains insufficiently defined or addressed; in other contexts it is excluded from the school curriculum, and we need to consider whether this is detrimental to the development of the affective dimension. How are those involved in work with children and young people prepared and equipped to face the levels of imagination, openness and creativity which they will encounter on a regular basis? Hart (2003, p.45) suggests that adults can help children develop discrimination by comparing notes and framing some simple questions: 'Which is the better choice? Is this person trustworthy? Which choice seems to have more light or flows better? With practice we can help children distinguish between "real feelings"… and the ego's tug.'

William James (1977, original work published 1902) described such feelings as ineffable – words cannot convey their meaning. A sense of awe and wonder and oneness reflects a sense of transcendence, of learning to be still and experiencing times of amazement and wonder: realizing that the self is important but that it is a part of something greater (Lealman 1996). Adults should help children keep an open mind, explore ways of seeing, encourage personal awareness and become personally aware of the social and political dimensions of spirituality (Hay and Nye 2006). Adults who are able to wonder alongside the children they care for open up free space in which mystery can be explored (Hart 2003). Indeed, Hart suggests the notion of the bliss station: a physical place or mental space where an individual is able to find peace, room to imagine and a sense of connectedness with something greater than themselves.

Maria, a community nurse in a suburban setting, recounts her experience of working with one young boy who used physical space to 'find himself':

> I shall never forget working with Jamie, aged 7, who was frequently tired and restless whenever he visited the clinic. At first I wondered whether I should be doing more to occupy him or attract his attention somehow, but I soon learned that his mother used to go out in the evening, locking the children in the house. She was unaware that Jamie would climb out of

his bedroom window onto the garage roof, climb down the drainpipe and spend the evening playing in the local park. By the time she returned home, late in the evening, he was exhausted but safe in bed.

Jamie was an energetic child whose learning, health and well-being were being impaired by his lifestyle. His identity was rooted in his love of fresh air: playing football, socializing, riding his bike and feeling free. His home and school life contrasted with this, bringing restrictions, rules and the need to conform. Even at such a young age, he knew the value of freedom and accessed the opportunities as they arose.

Adults also need to find that inner sense of self and to consider how they identify themselves.

> A group of adults engaged in an activity based on an experiential approach to learning. They each had a representation of a wardrobe, and could choose a selection of clothes with which to fill it. On each garment they named a role by which they were known, so that the cupboard came to represent who they were. People included roles such as employee, mother, parent, shopper, carer, artist, driver and sister. The participants were asked to choose the essential roles – and to weed out some clothes for storage (not to be thrown away, but to be stored safely as less important). This is a fascinating activity and one which helps one to consider *who am I?* On this occasion one participant said: 'I have all these names, but *where am I* in amongst all of this?'

The question, 'Who am I?' is often misinterpreted as, 'What do I do?' We have become *human doings* rather than *human beings*. The sense of being – and being allowed to be – is fundamental to gaining a sense of self that goes beyond human activity. It considers the heart of the person, rather than the role played by that person. This is not an easy concept, but it is one worth exploring; for it is in this sense of self that one may find an acceptance and security that are far deeper and more profound than a sense of identity that is established by activity and role. As adults we can consider what space (internal or external) we allow ourselves to consider such questions, and then, in turn, reflect on how we provide and support such opportunities with our children.

Developing clarity of vision

In the present climate, all too often we focus on what is measurable, logical or deductible, what is based in science or reason, at the expense of the direct knowing that can come from awareness of one's inner voice. Hart suggests that in effect adult society has grown a cataract over the eye of contemplation: it has made it cloudy with mistrust. However, most children still have clear vision: they are natural contemplatives (Hart 2003). Lang *et al.* (1994) reinforce this idea, suggesting that the development of children's learning is about far more than the cognitive. Education (in its widest sense) is concerned with the moral, the political and the affective. Indeed, education and the growth of the whole person are synonymous. Young children live at the limit of their experiences most of the time (Berryman 1985). They are continually encountering new situations and experiences. Thus they are repeatedly having to imagine new possibilities, take risks involving trial and error, and face up to new opportunities. They are exploring new possibilities and gaining a sense of themselves and their capabilities. Finding a sense of self is an essential part of childhood. Developing an understanding of what it means to be a member of one's family and community, and coming to understand how relationships work, including power relationships, is fundamental to establishing an outlook on the world and to sensing how one fits in. This sense of going through, over or beyond various limitations and obstacles is in essence the meaning of transcendence (Myers 1997). The very sense of being connected to others (whether people, creatures or things) is intangible, it goes beyond anything that is visible or tactile; it is, in essence, spiritual. These issues will be explored in relation to global citizenship in Chapter 6.

Violence, conflict and identity

The sense of self, and of being connected to others, is influenced by many factors. At times we define our selves in terms of power relationships and of how we perceive ourselves to be valued in comparison to others. A sense of powerlessness, frustration or of being oppressed will impact on our sense of self. The stereotypes and expectations associated with gender are one factor that affects our identity.

For many boys and men, risk-taking is among the few ways in which they can exert some form of power within a world in which they have very little influence (Mills 2001; Woolley 2007). In societies where masculinity has evolved over past decades, where men are no longer the breadwinners and where girls are outperforming boys in the education system (as is the case now in the UK), the traditional expectations about what it means to be male, and the accompanying stereotypes, need to be questioned and modified.

If we look at the example of contemporary South Africa, it would appear that the risks associated with sexual activity and violence may be subordinate to the ongoing traditional perception of a need for men to appear successful, sexually active and powerful. The way in which male identity is constructed is still heavily influenced by the legacy of apartheid. Families remain separated as the result of labour migration, which can lead to their disintegration. In addition, male identity (defined as it is, by issues of dominance, power and potency) is also affected significantly by the spread of the HIV/AIDS epidemic, fuelled by and linked to other factors like poverty, violence and the lack of education (Ruxton 2004). This has implications for health care and education in other contexts. Childcare professionals need to help children and young people to develop a sense of self-identity and self-respect that is not dependent upon a sense of power derived from sexual prowess (whether real, perceived or claimed) or the stereotypes associated with their gender. They also need to explore the idea that whilst some relationships do have a sexual element, this is only one facet of a relationship that includes the spiritual dimensions of friendship, mutual support, love and care (Woolley 2007).

The fact that residents of the KwaZulu Natal region of South Africa experience 40 per cent unemployment – and in northern areas as high as 60–70 per cent (Morrell 2005) – underlies the desperation and frustration experienced by some of the population. KwaZulu Natal has been one of the most violent areas in South Africa, with 50,000 people killed in the five years after the election of Nelson Mandela. Morrell argues that both education in non-violent behaviour and sex education need to start from the reception year in school. Because of the history of inequality and struggle in South Africa, men need to be encouraged to develop a sense of personal identity and to learn how to develop respectful and non-violent relationships with those around them. One of the greatest challenges is to show boys and girls that they can be friends and not just sexualized others (Morrell 2005). We will return to these issues in Chapter 4.

This example highlights the need for all children of primary school age to be enabled to develop a sense of self: self-identity, self-esteem and personal values. This enterprise has a spiritual dimension, for it requires that individual children gain a sense of who they are and begin to develop their view of how they fit into the world.

Sex education needs to involve much more than the transmission of knowledge. It needs to explore the emotions and to provide children and young people with opportunities to talk about love and intimacy. Children need to consider personal values such as forgiveness, sensitivity to others, faithfulness, loyalty, personal integrity, conscience and commitment (Halstead and Waite 2001). Exploring these issues will enable children and young people to develop positive relationships built upon trust and respect. It will also help to address some of the violence (whether physical or emotional) and power struggles that characterize some human relationships.

The existence of violence in the lives of children is explored by Montgomery, Burr and Woodhead (2003), Kehily and Swann (2003) and Miles and Wright (2003). Using photographs and children's drawings, Montgomery *et al.* present a fascinating introduction to the subject, exploring the nature of violence, how it is viewed in different settings, and issues around bullying. Their exploration of situations faced by child soldiers, which includes experiences recounted by young people, is particularly powerful. It addresses not only the situation in Cambodia under the Khmer Rouge and examples from Uganda and Burma, but also the position of those under the age of eighteen serving in the British Army. The contrasting contexts give breadth to the examination of the subject and challenge the reader's perceptions. The examination of the role of children in the struggle against apartheid in South Africa, and the detail about their treatment (Montgomery *et al.* 2003), presents a stark challenge to the assumption that children should not participate in fighting for a cause in which they believe. The view that such children had no choice but to make a stand against the injustice, brutality and mistreatment they faced is compelling.

Kehily and Swann (2003) begin to explore how conflict resolution is addressed in contrasting cultures. They observe that in the UK, USA, Canada and Australia friendships are founded on a belief system that emphasizes personal autonomy and individuality. They contrast this with the traditional collectivist culture found in China, where the direct expression of feelings, the rejection of verbal aggression and the use of meditation all contribute to conflict avoidance. They are keen to avoid the use of over-generalizations, and signal the limited application of some research evidence, but still the contrast between traditionally Christian societies and those influenced by Buddhism, Taoism and Confucianism raises interesting questions for those involved with children and young people. Our understanding of relationships, and the Western focus on individuality and individual self-assertion, make it essential for us to support children in the development of a sense of being linked to those around them, both in their own communities and the wider world.

Having worked with primary school children (aged from three to eleven years) in areas of social and economic disadvantage in the UK, we believe that understanding the influence of local culture (particularly family values) upon the emerging ability of children to resolve conflict is an important part of the childcare professional's work. Where the home environment is founded on the need to seek revenge rather than resolution, and where parents and carers encourage their child to retaliate rather than to seek mediation in response to incidents of aggression or unfair play, childcare professionals have a responsibility to develop a culture rooted in collective responsibility and mutual support rather than individualism and personal survival.

The aims of one British school illustrate how such shared values can be fostered, and are based on the acrostic REACT:

- **R**espect differences
- **E**veryone matters
- **A**im high
- **C**elebrate success
- **T**ogether

These values are supported by focusing on the word TEAM (**T**ogether **E**veryone **A**chieves **M**ore). This focus on collective well-being, balanced with developing a sense of personal uniqueness and achievement, contrasts with the dominant focus on the individual in contemporary Western societies. Where the response to conflict is retaliation in order to assert one's individuality and power, the coherence of humanity as a whole is undermined. This school is seeking to address issues of interconnectedness and to use them in order to promote acceptance, cooperation and harmony. In essence, it is seeking to nurture spiritual connections between children, and others, involved in the school.

It is not only in the school that such connections can have an impact. Kehily and Swann (2003) point to the possible influence of the extended family upon children's friendships. They observe that where children live in multi-generational homes they encounter compromise on a frequent basis. This experience transfers onto their relationships outside the home, and upon their friendships with peers. Indeed, these children demonstrate superior skill at negotiation and compromise. This observation challenges us to consider how our children encounter inter-generational relationships, particularly in settings where families are geographically dispersed.

Children's voices: Challenging conflict

The roads to conflict resolution are many and depend significantly on the context in which the conflict arises. Montgomery asks whether children have a place in challenging oppression and exploitation when it impacts directly upon their everyday lives. Whether this comes through the oppressive practices of an immoral regime, or through the behaviour of the school bully on the playground, the answer must surely be 'yes'. Part of children's process of finding their voice and their identity is being able to identify fairness and to empathize with others. But the action necessary to challenge and change these circumstances need not involve significant risk on the part of the children themselves. Rather, it is the responsibility of the adults who care for these children to work on their behalf towards conflict resolution, fairness and peace and to ensure that the systems are in place to enable the children to access support and mediation. For some in the school system this will involve the development of a counter-culture, standing in contrast to the predominant culture of individual self-assertion outside.

Only in the most desperate circumstances, where there is no responsible adult, should the child resort to taking direct action. Our responsibility as childcare professionals, and as parents and carers, is to create a sanctuary – a place with clear values, expectations and procedures. The importance of involving children in consultation so that their opinions are considered as relevant and influential in the development of such an environment is fundamental to community-centred interventions (Miles and Wright 2003). Again, this is a part of the 'scaffolding' role of the adult.

The idea of tough self-sufficiency may be admired in some people, but children who assume such a façade can lose contact with their more genuine feelings of vulnerability, dependency and need for relationship (Hay and Nye 2006). The danger is that we become a society which is geared to exploitation and division, rather than to healing and wholing (Lealman 1996). But what sort of experiences can help children and young people to have a sense of belonging, of being a part of society and of feeling united with others, resulting in increased trust, gentleness and empathy?

> Working with children at the time of the fall of the Berlin Wall (in 1989), Peter was interested to hear their responses to the idea of divided worlds: 'We discussed the notion of a wall separating us from a different, unknown, place. "If there was an ideal world on the other side of the wall – what would it be like?" I asked. Jody suggested that: "It would be a place without any suffering or illness, where my Granddad was well and fit and able to play." Matthew said: "The houses would have gardens with no [intravenous drug] needles or old condoms."'

These aspirations, from children of 10 and 11 years of age, present a challenge to any hearer. For children to raise such issues shows their awareness of the needs within their own communities, their own longing for change and a sense of hope.

McLaughlin (1996) speaks of the need to develop a wider moral ecology beyond one's own individual and individualistic tendencies, encompassing a social ethos, a consensus on the common good and notions of loyalty and responsibility to the community. Imagining our ideal world, as Peter enabled his children to do, helps us to consider how we might wish to change this present world. Providing such opportunities to begin to voice these aspirations is a first step to challenging unfair, violent and unjust practices in our own lives and our societies.

Finding the self: Creativity and unexpected opportunities

Of course, moments of self-realization do not always come through planned activities or discussion starters. Sometimes they appear at the most unexpected moment, and at times their meaning is only understood with the benefit of hindsight. A primary school teacher, Robert, recalls an incident which draws together many aspects that have been discussed in this chapter so far:

> Early in my career, I introduced my class to printing. We cut patterns and pictures into linoleum blocks and produced two-tone designs. Shane developed a representation of a railway locomotive using yellow and black ink. The result was attractive and appealing; I still have a copy. At the end of the lesson Shane would not clear his materials away. In the end I cleared up for him, but he sat with the sharp linoleum cutter in his hand, picking away at the block all through the time when I read the end-of-day story. To say that I was nervous would be an understatement. He was sitting next to my desk with a sharp tool, appearing to be frustrated or angry, and throughout my reading I wondered what he might do with his frustration – presumably felt as a result of me ending the lesson. Needless to say, he went home peacefully at the end of the day, having cleared away the remainder of his equipment. With hindsight I have gained a sense of how much he enjoyed the lesson, that he felt a sense of creativity and freedom of expression, and that he wanted to carry on when I ended the activity. As he left my classroom he turned back and gave me his artwork. I thought he would want to take it home to show his family, but he was insistent that I should keep it. This is why I have always kept it; as a reminder of the day when he enjoyed being in school and expressing himself.

We conjecture that Shane had an experience which far outstripped Robert's expectations for the lesson – one that went beyond learning skills and processes. He was absorbed in the activity, found enjoyment, created a unique piece of art and felt satisfaction. He was absorbed in his own sense of being and had an ineffable experience. That he could not end the activity in the way required raises issues of how we structure activities with children and how we identify and address those moments when something special or precious has occurred.

Some recommendations

- We need to balance opportunities for spiritual experience (awe and wonder, reflection, imagining and silence) with our other expectations and requirements of children.

- An appreciation of the inner self can help to develop self-esteem and self-identity which lead to a reduction in, and resolution of, conflict.

- Adults need to consider how starting points can be used with children to encourage questioning and to value their natural fascination and enquiry.

- We need to consider how we identify ourselves. Is it through *being* or *doing*?

- It is essential for adults to take time to be quiet. Do we have a 'bliss station' – whether within ourselves or a special place to which we like to withdraw? This can enable us to be effective role models for children.

Conclusion

The spiritual dimension of childhood is not measurable against criterion-referenced attainment targets or inspection criteria; it may be difficult to quantify, but this does not negate its importance. It may be ethereal and ineffable, yet it is an essential and intrinsic part of developing a sense of self and an understanding of one's place in the world. Developing a sense of being, rather than doing, and making connections with others at a range of levels, provides the foundation on which to build positive relationships based around empathy, care, mutual understanding and kindness. If adults are able to scaffold such opportunities for children, and to value their own spiritual dimension, then both adults and children will develop further the sense of self and voice that help personal identity to evolve.

PART II
Children's Worlds

CHAPTER 3

Children's Worlds: The Variety of Spiritual Experience

Already in this book, we have glimpsed the many facets of children's spiritual experience. We have heard talk, albeit briefly, of children seeing people who have died, of encounters with angels, of dreams which make an impact, and of being lost in one's own world, creating new places and characters out of materials to hand. These instances indicate some of the different types of experiences that children have which may be termed 'spiritual'. In this chapter we explore examples, drawn from literature from different disciplines in different countries, to illustrate the range of experiences which children have. Some of these you will have encountered yourself. Others you may never have thought of as spiritual. Some may be new to you. But where possible, these narratives are recounted in the children's words in order to convey as fully as possible the ways in which the children experienced them, became absorbed in them, reflected upon them, or carried them along on their journey into adulthood. Above all, the challenge for you during this chapter is to immerse yourself in the spiritual lives of children. However, this is not necessarily an easy task.

Despite the fact that we were all once children, it can be difficult to recapture those feelings and worldviews which shaped us at a young age. Naturally we forget many such details over the years. Who has not been embarrassed by their parents, who like to impress their audiences with tales of how, when young, we used to believe that the moon was made of cheese or believed we could make ourselves invisible? But for the child, the world can be a magical place in which anything is possible, and that is something easily forgotten as we become adults and inhabit a more rational, scientific world dominated by timetables and practicalities. Whilst we rush around, however, many children are regularly encountering spiritual moments – ones which we can easily miss.

This chapter explores the wide variety of experiences which some may term 'spiritual'. The title of this chapter is loosely based on the title of William

James' book, *The Varieties of Religious Experience*, in which he detailed the rich-ness and diversity of religious experience. This chapter offers such an approach to the spiritual. It presents children's experiences under subhead-ings which are not intended to be definitive. Indeed, many overlap with each other, but by using subheadings it is not our intention to list every type of encounter possible, nor to rigidly categorize them. Rather, it is our aim to offer you signposts on the path to recognizing and nurturing children's spirituality in the varied forms it can take.

Moments of awe and wonder

Awe and wonder. When was the last time you felt awe and wonder? It may have been yesterday, or perhaps you cannot remember. If you fall into the lat-ter category it is quite understandable, as our lives are dominated by work and study, by rushing to meet constant deadlines and be at places at set times. It can feel as if there is no time to be silent, to take in our surroundings or marvel at the world around us. Yet in childhood, it can be different. Young children are constantly expressing wonder, asking questions, and are curious to see, touch, taste and smell everything around them. For some, such moments can be incredibly spiritual, as Daniel Scott discovered when he asked adults to describe childhood experiences which they perceived as being spiritual. Scott (2004) recounts the story of a Canadian woman, Joyce, who told of the night when she was three years old, when her older brother took her outside to see a full moon. She recalled how she had never realized before that night that the moon existed, but was 'astonished by its utter beauty and glimmering light'. Her brother explained how the moon and sun were big balls out in space, just as the earth was. Joyce felt a strong sense of connection with these three balls, and throughout her life felt she had 'been given a very precious gift: the moon the sun, the Earth,' which had 'fed, warmed and amazed' her since that night (Scott 2004, p.75).

Tobin Hart recounts a similar story of an eight-year-old girl named Miranda, who was on a beach with her father. Her father watched her as she stood in the sea, up to her waist, swaying with the tide as if she were in a trance. He watched and watched and time passed by, with Miranda standing in the sea for an hour and a half. Then she walked back onto the sand, with an aura of peace and calmness, and sat down next to her father, pausing before saying, 'I was the water…I was the water. I love it and it loves me. I don't know how else to say it' (Hart 2003, p.47).

As these examples show, children are particularly quick not only to take notice of nature, but to marvel at it and be inspired by it – but it can be easy to miss their responses in our busy world. Rebecca Nye describes the 'signature phenomenon' of children's spirituality, proposing that we need to consider each child's individual personal style if we are to hear their spirituality at all (Hay and Nye 2006, p.97). Such signatures are not simplistic; they do not rely solely on a child's religious background, gender, age or position in a family. Nye offers an example similar to that of Joyce, with an account of an articulate six-year-old called Ruth, who also experienced moments of awe and wonder with regard to nature. When asked what made her think of God, Ruth said, 'When I see um…the trees burst into life. In spring I like that. But when I see the lambs in Wales, oh…it makes me…oh…leap and jump too!' (*ibid.* p.95). Nye comments that Ruth's signature, which ran through their conversations, was characterised by an aesthetic appreciation of the natural world.

Seeing and sensing

The awe and wonder experienced by children often incorporates a sense of mystery or the mysterious in what they see. Elaine Champagne (2001), a chaplain in Canada, describes the story of a two-and-a-half-year old girl called Katie, who became captivated by a feather whilst playing on the beach. Katie spent a long time looking at it and touching it before placing it on the water and watching it bob backwards and forwards with the tide. She then reached for it again, picked it up and continued to play with it, becoming absorbed in it for almost half an hour.

The two adults who were with Katie, watching her during this time, were moved by her wonder at this feather and the ocean, and how it had absorbed her so completely. Champagne (2001) analyses the incident further, suggesting that the girl was exploring, wondering and contemplating. Of course, Katie's fascination with the feather also places her experience in the 'awe and wonder' category – which demonstrates how these categories overlap. Likewise, knowledge of her other spiritual experiences – not documented by Champagne – might also indicate the signature of an aesthetic appreciation of the natural world, as defined by Nye (Hay and Nye 2006). Hay and Nye also write of 'mystery sensing' – which again encompasses the awe, wonder and fascination that absorb children as they interact with the world and universe – as well as the questions which emanate from those interactions.

Moments such as these are obviously visible to the adult's naked eye. If we take the time to watch, we can regularly observe children engaging in such moments with nature. They are examples of what we have already touched upon in this book – examples of the spiritual manifesting in the ordinary moments of daily life. Other such instances can lie in something as simple as rolling in the autumn leaves, creating a snowman, or being lost in a piece of music. When asked if he had ever been aware of a presence or power different from his everyday self, a 14-year-old boy living in the UK responded: 'I sometimes feel like this when I listen to a particularly moving piece of music' (Little, no date, p.12). To the observer, a young person in his situation would perhaps be seen as simply enjoying listening to a piece of music, but for this boy there were additional feelings associated with it.

Many instances of children seeing and sensing may not necessarily be evident to adults, because they can involve seeing something that is not visible to adults. Often, adults' awareness depends on the child verbalizing their experience so that adults become aware of it, as in the case of the young man listening to music. Hart's (2003) six-year-old daughter would tell her parents how she saw shapes and colours around people and objects – something the parents would otherwise have been unaware of. When asked how she saw them, she explained, pointing to her forehead, that she saw them from inside rather than with her eyes, indicating an awareness of what the Hindu tradition calls the 'third eye' (Hart 2003, p.123). In another case, also recounted by Hart, a young girl was found dancing around her bedroom as if trying to catch something in the air. She explained that she was catching lights that were sprinkling down from the ceiling, after having awoken to see wires of color around her. Without these children describing these colours, their parents would have remained unaware of their experience.

It is also important to note that in some cases, despite the best attempts to verbalize an experience, words cannot always convey them adequately. This is particularly true of experiences which involve a sensory perception of the spiritual. A twelve-year-old Christian girl in the UK commented that sometimes she felt a force pushing her to do something good, such as help others, but that this force wasn't a physical one, but one which she couldn't 'really describe' (Little, no date, p.12). The sensing of a presence or of something greater than oneself is a frequent occurrence in moments of spirituality. Hay and Nye (2006) conceptualize this as 'awareness sensing', whereby children respond to the present moment, being alert to the experience of what might occur in those moments of stillness or silence. Awareness of the senses is explored further in Chapter 4.

The afterlife

In Chapter 1 we heard how children's voices can be confident, inquisitive and uninhibited when exploring death and the issues which surround it – often in contrast to adults' voices. Even if you are unsettled by the thought of reading more about death, children regularly report spiritual experiences which are related to death. They are often meaningful for many children, helping them to seek answers and find meaning about life, and as an adult, you need to be prepared to engage with children on this topic if they so desire. As we mentioned in Chapter 1, for many adults death is a difficult subject to deal with. However, children will not only ask questions about death but may also report encounters with the deceased – encounters which they are usually quite 'matter-of-fact' about. In some instances, children report seeing or having conversations with the deceased person just as they would have done prior to the death. Jean, a mother living in England, told of how her son Paul entered the living room one evening when he was six years old.

> 'Have you been playing?' Jean asked her son.
> 'No,' he replied calmly. 'I was sitting on the stairs talking to Grandma.'
> Paul then picked up a story book and asked his mum to read it to him.

Paul's grandmother had died some months before. Jean, who was open to the idea of an afterlife, was comforted by Paul's experience, and relieved that he had not been frightened by it in any way. Interestingly, Paul did not continue the conversation with his mother by asking any questions about the incident. It appeared that he was fully accepting of the fact that his grandmother had been there, even though he knew that she had died.

In psychological terms, seeing a person who has died is conceptualized as part of the grieving process. Essentially, following bereavement, there are recognized phases which people move through, although not necessarily in a linear progression. The first is a feeling of numbness, which is characterized by shock or denial of the death. Another phase is of disorganization, in which a wide range of emotions are experienced, including fear, anger, guilt, relief and a sense of searching for the deceased. A third phase is one of reorganization in which the bereaved is able to readjust, treasure memories of the deceased and begin to emotionally reinvest in life (Garfield 1996). One aspect of the denial of the death can be manifested in seeing the deceased person, perhaps in the street, on a train or in a crowd of people.

However, children (as well as adults) see deceased people not only in the course of waking life; many see them in dreams. Some dreams can be an intensely spiritual experience – a phenomenon noted in ancient civilizations, and Chapter 8 is devoted to this. Some of these spiritual dreams are related to death, and include visiting heaven, and/or seeing deceased people and pets again, and many of them bring comfort to the dreamer. Claire, an 11-year-old girl living in Britain, explained how a friend of hers had died when they were both eight years old. One night she dreamt that there was 'this big golden tunnel and I was walking through it and she was at the end of it and, em, she was there and I was just talking to her and I says, "What's happening?"' The girls continued to have a brief conversation, during which her friend described how she was happy with new friends and Claire told her about events at school, before the dream ended. Claire thought that the tunnel was the 'gate to heaven' (Adams and Hyde 2008).

The dream made a considerable impact upon Claire, offering her reassurance that her friend was still alive, and also a sense of happiness that they had been able to see each other, because it had 'been a long time' since they had. In psychological terms, the dream may indicate that Claire was in the latter stages of grieving. As Mallon (2005) suggests, dreams in which the deceased person visits the dreamer can indicate that the bereaved person has moved from disbelief to acceptance. This acceptance may also be indicated by Claire's reassurance that her friend was well. Whilst Claire could have viewed the dream as one which simply brought back memories of her friend, she appears to have made meaning from the golden tunnel and the conversation the girls had. As Fisher (1999), Bosacki (2001), Tacey (2003) and Hyde (2004) have noted, for some people connectedness with a transcendent dimension is an aspect of spirituality. For Claire, the dream certainly had religious connotations and dealt with issues of life after death. Rather than simply perceiving the dream as a combination of images derived from memories of her friend and ideas of what the gates to heaven might be like, Claire found meaning which also embodied a transcendent dimension (Adams and Hyde 2008).

Ultimate questions

All children will inevitably ask adults about death. In their young lives they will be confronted with the death of perhaps a pet or an elderly relative, or in a smaller number of cases, the death of a parent or carer, sibling or friend. But, as Hyde (2008) shows, explorations of death and what might lie beyond are often a part of children weaving threads of meaning in order to connect with those who have died. Writing in the context of an Australian rural town, Hyde notes how Kristy wondered about why people die and go to heaven, and about what they might do there. Emily wondered about why her uncle died at a young age, whilst her grandpa lived to be quite elderly before dying. Emily further commented that she wished she could have known her grandpa in a more intimate way before he died. This was perhaps indicative of such a longing for connection.

However, it is not simply about death that children ask. Often they probe other philosophical aspects of life, asking what can be described as ultimate questions, as the example of Jane illustrates.

> Jane is three years old. Her family is having dinner together one evening and is chatting about some of the antics that Michael – Jane's older brother, who is now nine years old – got up to when he was younger. Jane listens intently as her mother recounts the time when Michael was playing in the backyard and got himself stuck in the branch of the large elm tree. All of the members of the family laugh heartily. Jane is hanging on every word that her mother says. She seems to be captivated by this story. When the laughing has subsided, Jane turns to her mother and asks, 'Where was I when Michael got stuck in the tree?' Jane's mother looks lovingly at her and replies, 'You weren't born then, sweetheart.' But Jane's wonder and curiosity have been aroused, and she has a sense of connection to something greater. Insistently, she pursues the conversation. 'Yes, I know,' persists Jane, 'but, *where was I?*' (as told by Hyde 2008).

Hart (2003) cites a similar example of a seven-year-old American boy named John who asked his father why he (John) was here, on earth. The question was posed during a trip to a shop to buy food – an excellent example of how children's deep thinking can be expressed in seemingly unrelated contexts, again alerting adults to the need to listen out for such spiritual ponderings.

Children are naturally inquisitive, and regularly pose such questions in the course of exploring their meaning and purpose in life. In essence, they ask the questions which we have all asked, and which many of us continue to ask, particularly in light of personal or world tragedies: Why is the human race here? Is there life before physical birth, or after physical death? Why do innocent people suffer? Is there a God? Why do war and poverty continue to plague the world? Hart (2003, p.91) describes children as 'natural philosophers', always ready to seek answers to life's big questions.

As children become older, they naturally develop their views in light of cognitive, social and emotional development, but that does not dilute the richness of their thoughts. A thirteen-year-old agnostic boy in the UK explained how his views had changed. 'When I was little I used to believe in reincarnation and about heaven and hell. But if there was a heaven and hell, everyone would go to hell, because no one can live their life without doing something bad' (Draycott and Blaylock, no date, p.21). This boy's views had changed over the years, having moved from believing in reincarnation to now hovering between two ideas – sometimes believing that death was the end, and sometimes believing that if a person had 'unfinished business' there would be an opportunity to 'finish it'. As with many children, this boy's thoughts were partly shaped by ideas found in world religions – for example, concepts of heaven and hell and of reincarnation. But it is important to note that children do not necessarily frame all of their opinions in the tradition in which they may have been raised. Jane, cited above, who had a strong sense of herself having existed before she was in her mother's womb, was raised in a Catholic tradition, yet her intuitive sense was of a pre-existence, akin to an Eastern philosophy of reincarnation.

For many children such searching can be seen in the context of their spirituality – a quest for their sense of identity, which we explored in depth in Chapter 2, and will later in the book. This development of a sense of purpose helps to foster a positive identity and a sense of being a part of something far greater than themselves. For adults, the role of engaging in these often challenging conversations with children is a pivotal one, even if the child seems to be contradicting the beliefs held within the family unit. As part of the search for identity, many of the questions children raise, and the spiritual experiences they have, strongly relate to their relationships with self, others, the world, and sometimes a transcendent other – which Hay and Nye (2006) include in their definition of relational consciousness.

Religious experience

Questions about a possible afterlife, and asking philosophical questions, can also be encounters with the religious for some people. As we discussed in the introduction and in Chapter 1, some religious experiences can be spiritual in the eyes of the child who experienced it, and/or in the eyes of the observer. Equally, some experiences can be spiritual without being religious. It can, for example, be argued that seeing a person who has died can be a spiritual experience. If the child who is seeing is from a religious background and believes that people go to heaven or are reincarnated after bodily death, then such an experience can also be a religious one, possibly confirming their faith in an afterlife as taught in a religious tradition. Conversely, a person may believe in life after death but not align themselves to any religious tradition, and so may not claim that the experience has been a religious one. Hence, there will be overlap with other headings in this chapter. It is this issue of perception which leads us to consider some experiences which are both religious and spiritual in the eyes of the children who report them.

In the 1980s the Warwick Religions and Education Research Unit at the University of Warwick, UK, began a longitudinal, ethnographic study into religious experience of children and young people. Whilst religious nurture was the primary concern of the analysis, spirituality was also a focus.

> Eleanor Nesbitt (2001) describes the case of Mina, a Gujurati, who was interviewed at the ages of 12 and 21. When 12, Mina was deeply involved in the activities of a group of devotees of Sathya Sai Baba, a spiritual leader living in India. Nesbitt observed how Mina held a strong enthusiasm for life, excitedly taking part in religious ceremonies and describing meaningful experiences. At 21, Mina was a psychology student, and at this time of her life distinguished between religion and spirituality. Now, whilst she still believed in Sai Baba's teachings, she no longer practised any religion, preferring instead to follow 'a more universal way... [to] reach the same destination'. She described how for her an intense feeling of 'total peace' had been a spiritual experience, but this was strongly aligned to her religious belief in God (Nesbitt 2001, p.135). For Mina, religion had played a very strong part in her upbringing and it was only in her years as a young woman that she began to differentiate between religion and spirituality. But irrespective of the label she assigned to experiences such as the feeling of total peace, they were significant ones which she could articulate clearly, even at a young age.

For children in all communities throughout the world, religion may influence their spirituality. Coles (1990) talked to a girl, Natalie, from the Hopi community in North America. Central to the Hopi belief system is the concept of connectedness with their ancestors. Natalie explained how she often, in her thoughts, met with her ancestors who would give her a blanket, hold her and point to the sky, telling her there were more ancestors above them. She explained to Coles how the ancestors visit and whisper to the elderly people in the community, and how the elderly then passed on the wisdom of the conversations to the children. This contact with the ancestors may be also considered a religious experience, as defined by the Hopi community.

> Coles (1990) also talked to Ilona, an eleven-year-old Jewish girl living on the east coast of the USA. She talked of what her Jewish faith meant to her, and spoke of her closeness to God. She talked in the context of her father's job, which involved significant amounts of international travel by air. On occasions he had been able to take Ilona with him and she explained how he would point out cities, rivers and mountains from the aeroplane windows. She described how when she was on a plane she felt nearer to God, 'because you can see the world, a lot of it, more than you

can see when you're on land, and you can realize how big the whole universe is'. For Ilona, it was always important to pause once in a while and reflect on God. She explained how it was important to remember the teachings of God, given through Moses, 'because it's the big picture that counts, and if you forget that, you get lost in going from one place to another, because you don't think of what you should be doing for God' (as told by Coles 1990, p.255).

Ilona made explicit reference to her scriptural teachings in the course of her conversations, reflecting her upbringing. Naturally, this will be a common feature of many religious children's accounts.

Habib, a twelve-year-old Muslim boy living in Tunisia, also referred to his religion's teachings. He talked eloquently of his connection to Allah and how, when he heard the *adhan,* the call to prayer, he would stop everything and say to Allah, 'I'm only this one boy, but I believe in you.' He continued, 'Sometimes the wind is strong, and I think I'll be picked up and carried away!' because for Habib, 'Allah hears prayers and answers them through the wind' (as told by Coles 1990, p.199).

The children in this section, from a variety of different faith and cultural backgrounds, clearly demonstrate how some experiences can be both religious and spiritual, and how children can use religious language to express them. In our increasingly globalized world, it is important to recognize the different ethnic and faith backgrounds of the children in our care, and be aware that their spiritual language may be influenced by their religious upbringing. You may not initially possess knowledge of their particular faith, but gaining an understanding of it will help you to understand the children's experiences in more depth.

The darker sides of spiritual experience

Until now, the language of this book has largely been positive when discussing children's spirituality – those moments of awe, wonder, fascination and insight... Indeed, these terms are highly appropriate, but it would be wrong to imply that all spiritual moments are so gentle, touching and poignant. In fact, whilst spiritual experiences often involve children reflecting on their identity and inner self, and can lead to personal growth, the experiences may be less than comfortable for both child and listener.

Hay and Nye (2006) relate the story of Tim, a ten-year-old boy, which exemplifies this point. When discussing Tim's 'signature', the authors

CHILDREN'S WORLDS: THE VARIETY OF SPIRITUAL EXPERIENCE 69

describe it as one of inner struggle. When discussing questions of whether or not there was a God, or how we can cope with the mystery of infinity, Tim's answers were characterized by conflicting hypotheses and frustration. He battled with conflicting arguments and could not settle on any one point of view. When Tim talked of his experiences which could be defined as spiritual, such as feelings experienced at sacred sites, his language was very much negative. For example, 'he used words such as "spooky", "shiver" and "cold" in a manner consistent with his overall framework and disposition' (Hay and Nye 2006, p.97). Although these moments were special to him, they were also balanced by a sense of struggle as to the level of their validity. In some ways, it may be that Tim found the search for his own identity a struggle – battling with conflicting arguments in the search for his own opinions and explanations for experiences, which would form part of who he was.

Inevitably we need to return momentarily to the theme of death. Whilst the instances related to the afterlife recounted above gave comfort to the children, reassuring them that there was something more beyond this world, not all encounters will be so pleasurable. Joe, a nine year old boy living in Scotland, explained:

> I was sitting on my bed reading a book one night. My mum and dad were downstairs and were watching TV. I was supposed to be asleep but I wasn't tired so I got my book out but suddenly I jumped as my door creaked. I thought Dad was coming in and would catch me reading so I dropped the book on the floor so he wouldn't see it. I heard Dad's footsteps coming into the room so I peeped over my blanket but I couldn't believe my eyes. It wasn't Dad, it was my uncle's ghost. I screamed like I had never screamed before. I had never been so frightened in my life.

For Joe, seeing his deceased uncle was far from being a reassuring experience. His terminology – 'ghost'– in itself conveyed his fear. Rather than saying he had seen his uncle, instead he used a word which can have supernatural, scary overtones for children. Whilst some of Joe's shock was related to having expected to see his father, he subsequently explained that for him, ghosts were 'things that haunt you'. He had not yet formulated beliefs about the afterlife, other than having ideas that ghosts were trapped in a zone somewhere between earth and heaven – an idea he appeared to have gained from television programmes.

> Having heard Joe scream, his parents naturally rushed to his room. Joe told them what had happened and his parents consoled him. Joe's mother

explained, 'I am sure it was just his imagination, but it really frightened him. Personally his father and I do not have strong beliefs about life after death either way, but we thought it important to talk to Joe about what he thought as it had clearly distressed him. The conversation seemed to help him, as he calmed down after a while and settled off to sleep.'

Joe's story highlights the potentially frightening or unsettling nature of some spiritual experiences. It is necessary to be alert to these, for children who have them will need additional support and comfort. For some, these darker moments will be forgotten, but often they can have a lasting effect upon children's thoughts and views. In Joe's case, he developed a belief system based on ghosts inhabiting the world, who are invisible to most people. Influenced by television programmes and films, Joe later began to tell his parents how ghosts were the spirits of people who couldn't yet travel to their final destination. They were, he said, trapped in a part of this world but were there also to help us. Some months after seeing the ghost of his uncle, he explained to his mother that his uncle had come into his room not to frighten him but to take care of Joe, by 'checking that he was alright'. In this way, he had made peace with the experience, although not all children will be able to do so.

Some recommendations

- One of the purposes of this chapter has been to highlight to you the range of spiritual experiences that occur in children's lives. One reason for this is to illuminate the diversity of experiences which are reported, for without that awareness, we may miss children's spiritual moments, or their attempts to share them with us. As Champagne (2001) says, we need not only to listen *to* their spiritual experiences, but also listen *for* them.

- In Chapter 1 we emphasized the need to listen carefully to the child who is telling his or her experience. As Scott (2001) suggests, it is important to listen to the spiritual narrative. An essential part of this process is to give the narrator respect, and to understand that their tale may have multiple functions. In sharing, the narrator may be, for example, trying to make sense of the experience themselves, make links to other parts of their life, or acknowledge the power it has had on their life.

- Not all spiritual experiences will be 'cute and fluffy'. Some are unsettling. Adults cannot ignore the less comfortable instances, for they, too, are significant to the child. Children will need extra support if they share such experiences, and it may be that in these cases they will need more than a listening ear, and will need to engage in reflective conversation about the issues in hand. Only the adult and the context in which the issues are raised can determine whether simply an ear, or an ear and a conversation, is required.

- Be aware that at times the boundaries between the religious and the spiritual may be blurred. For some people, the label given to the experience is important, for others it is not; as the observer or listener, simply be aware of the sensitivities of the issues of definition raised.

- Children, as natural philosophers, will regularly ask probing questions about the meaning of life. It may be tempting to run and hide, for such questions have no simple answers. But for many children, this searching is an expression of their spirituality – a searching for identity, meaning and purpose. Do not pretend to know answers to questions which you don't know – but encourage and join them on their philosophical quest.

- Words cannot always express the feelings and thoughts which accompany a spiritual experience, so do not pressurize children to articulate them. McCreery (1996) advocates the use of the children's own language, and in her own work with young children, she was careful to avoid the use of explicitly religious language.

- Finally, be aware that some children will also wish to keep their thoughts private, and this is to be respected.

Conclusion

This chapter has recounted different types of experiences which may be defined as spiritual. Where possible, the children's own words have been used in order to convey to readers a sense of how the experience impacted upon the child. In so doing, we have given children the spiritual voice which they often struggle to find, as we described in Chapter 1. To reiterate the points made in the opening of this chapter, this account of the variety of spiritual experience is not intended to be definitive, and the categorizations are neither fixed nor exhaustive. Rather, they are a continuation of our geography of the spiritual world, and are additional signposts for that journey.

CHAPTER 4

Connecting to Something Greater: Spirituality and Respect for Personhood

This chapter is concerned with some difficult questions of life and living. It aims to stimulate discussion and highlight key issues to help those involved with children, and ultimately the children to whom they relate, to consider the notion of personhood. Finding one's place in the world is essentially a spiritual journey: it requires the development of a sense of self-respect as well as the ability to respect others in one's community and the wider world. Children need to be supported in developing their own views on difficult issues and to understand that people's circumstances, needs and views are often shaped by contexts very different from their own. They also need to consider how taking risks affects them and those to whom they relate.

It is important for those working with children to be prepared to face the issues that children will raise: issues of life and death, of developing healthy relationships, of dealing with loss and grief, and of living a life informed by a positive sense of self-esteem and respect for oneself and for others. Each one relates to the child's sense of personhood and their understanding and valuing of the personhood of others; each one can be felt very deeply by children; each supports their sense of being a part of something far greater than themselves and stands in marked contrast to the individualism that so often characterizes contemporary Western societies.

The chapter begins with a consideration of the senses and how we understand them. It uses children's writing to explore their insights and perceptions and considers how a sense of feeling can help us to interpret and understand the world around and within us. Later, using the issue of HIV / AIDS education as a focus, this chapter explores how children can be supported in developing their own values, attitudes and understanding of respect. It uses issues from South Africa to help to stimulate debate about wider educational provision in other contexts and to explore what may be learned from this situation. This will enable readers to address their own preconceptions and values and to develop a vision for facing issues with children in their own situations. Whilst there is a particular focus on schools in this chapter, the issues raised will apply to any setting where children will ask questions and encounter controversial issues.

Sensing and feeling: Developing perception

The sense of feeling, of appreciating emotion, sensitivity, care, kindness, love and even sensuality, is an important element in the nurturing of spirituality. When one talks with children about *the senses* it is all too easy to fall into the trap of the factual: that there are five senses, based on experiencing the physical world through taste, touch, sight, smell and sound. Our work with children and young people needs to make clear that these are *only* five of the senses, and that although these may be experienced in concrete ways (which are interpreted by the individual) there are also myriad abstract senses which enable us to engage with and to interpret the world around us.

We may talk of feeling scared or lonely, of feeling elated and excited, yet these feelings are not always classified within the senses as they are presented to children. Helping children to understand that it is important to sense these feelings – as they help us to interpret the world, sometimes enhance our enjoyment of it and often keep us from danger – is an important part of their development. At times, it is difficult to identify why such feelings arise. We may feel *butterflies* or a *knot* in our stomach or a *tingle* down our spine. We are sensing something that informs the way in which we interpret the moment, and such a sense is not always easy to explain. These senses contribute to our sensing as a whole and help us to read situations.

We suggest that, as adults, we can help children to appreciate the wider senses. In fact it is essential that we nurture this understanding and show that sensing feelings is important and valid: we can scaffold the child's experience and expression of feelings, as was discussed in Chapter 2. It can be too easy to presume that children know the language of feeling. As adults we may presume what it means to be happy, sad, angry or elated. However, we can deepen our own understanding by discussing feelings with children and in turn enable them to develop their emotional awareness.

We worked with one group of children to discuss what feelings meant to them. They developed a selection of abstract noun poems to share their ideas. The poems reveal some interesting insights into their interpretations:

Anger is a little fierce creature that you do not want to be around.
Anger is like being thrown into a volcano.
Anger is like a fierce lion coming towards you;
It leaps up on you when the sky turns grey.
Anger empties your stomach; it makes you disappointed.

Mark, aged 10

Some say that Anger is a storm,
And some say it is a devil,
Some say it makes all wars start,
And some say it is all madness.

Some say that Anger is an eagle
And some say it is a deadly disease,
Some one across the road said
It is like a friend leaving you.

Simon, aged 10

Some say that Peace is calm and relaxing
And some say it takes your problems away.
Some say it makes your heart glow
And some say it is utter madness.

Does it look like a jigsaw muddled up?
Or does it look like an angel?
Does it stick with you all the way?
Or does it wave goodbye?

Katherine, aged 11

The children's writing shows an understanding of emotions that goes beyond the tangible or the physical senses. You may well wonder at some of the meaning, and may wish to take time to reflect. What the poems do suggest is that there is a deeper understanding of emotion than one might anticipate. As childcare professionals, or parents and carers, we are often engaged in helping children and young people to manage their anger or to consider what might make them happy. Counsellors will have more experience in this area than many others, but we are all engaged with children who feel a range of emotions, and have the opportunity to help them to understand their inner selves more fully.

The poems may make us reflect: what is anger, and what is peace? What are they to us? We may take for granted that these concepts are universally understood, yet this stifles the exploration of what the emotions are, how they feel, where they stem from and how they impact upon our lives. Adults can support this process by modelling the sharing of emotions and allowing children to see that it is acceptable to feel and to express those feelings; we can also model experiencing feelings that are difficult or impossible to express, and wanting to keep our feelings private. It is this far greater sense of feeling that begins to scratch below the surface of the human condition. In similar ways, we may speak of abstract concepts such as respect, fairness and empathy with children. Again, it is essential to consider what such notions involve and to learn from one another so that we understand our inner voice or apprehension.

Feelings about oneself

Feelings are not limited to the ways in which we react to the world around us; they also appertain to a sense of self: feelings of self-worth and self-esteem. The ways in which we care about ourselves, make healthy choices and feel positive about who we are, all affect our behaviours. Sometimes, these feelings lead to risky behaviours or to choices which cause us harm.

Children, young people and adults may engage in risky behaviours for a variety of reasons:

- seeking thrills and excitement
- disobeying authority
- asserting independence and self-identity
- occupying themselves when other activities are not available
- a lack of self-esteem or sense of self-worth.

Children may play by the local railway line because it gives a thrill and sense of excitement, it is a place to test one's own limits and courage, it is somewhere where they can find their own space (and thus identity) as no one else is allowed there, the area is a forbidden zone and is thus enchanting, and there may be few other places to play without the interference of others. There may also be an element of proving oneself to a group by engaging in a dangerous activity, and of gaining a place in a gang or friendship group. The adrenalin rush from the mixture of fear and excitement must also be a factor. It may also be a liminal place or bliss station (Hart 2003) where we can be ourselves and find peace and the opportunity for reflection.

The same principles can be applied to risk-taking behaviours such as the use of illegal drugs, playing with needles found in the street or park, or (for some older children) engaging in sexual activity, which may lead to many of the same feelings. As adults involved in work with children we are all aware of the need to promote a sense of safety and responsibility amongst our children: not only to advise them to leave needles and syringes where they find them, for example, but also to engender a sense of self-esteem that helps children to feel good about themselves without needing to take undue risks.

Allied to these risky behaviours is the possibility that one may become infected with HIV. In some contexts there is a significant focus on enabling children to keep themselves free from infection, in others HIV has less of a public profile and is not addressed with children. However, on a global scale this is an important issue and one that will be used in this chapter to provide the opportunity to explore issues surrounding personhood and self-esteem. Understanding that we are special and unique individuals, valued and valuable in the eyes of those around us, can enable us to begin to respect ourselves and to make sure that we take care of our own person and personality.

Addressing issues of HIV and AIDS with children of primary or elementary school age need not involve taking away any innocence about the sexualized world of adults. This loss of innocence is one of the main arguments offered by those opposed to teaching about HIV in schools. However, it can involve focusing on keeping safe and healthy and remembering how special we are. This sense of respect goes beyond the physical realm of science lessons and introduces the spiritual aspect: to understand that we are a part of something far greater than ourselves and that life is a precious thing to be valued and treated with care.

Exploring HIV/AIDS and a sense of personhood

A European Union survey (Eurobarometer 2006) found that over half of the Britons polled did not use protection to avoid HIV and 22 per cent believed HIV could be passed on by kissing, while just over half still thought you could become infected by sharing a glass. That such misconceptions still exist over twenty years after HIV/AIDS hit the headlines suggests that it is important to explore issues of HIV with children and young people, so that they begin to develop awareness and skills before risk taking occurs. It is important for us to consider the place and impact of such an exploration as a part of a child's journey of growth and learning.

Ever since the Department for Education (under various names over the years) began issuing circulars offering guidance on sex education in England, provision has been set in a context of children's spiritual and moral development (DES 1987; DfE 1994). In 2000, guidance stated that sex and relationship (sic) education should contribute to promoting the spiritual development of pupils at school (DfEE 2000). The change in terminology from 'sex education' to 'sex and relationship education' may have implied that the spiritual element of human relationships should be included in teaching. It is interesting to note that 'relationship' was presented in the singular, although many will encounter more than one relationship in their lifetime. However, there is no evidence that a spiritual dimension to sex education has permeated through to policymaking and planning at the level of the local authority or the individual school (Halstead and Waite 2001): 'A common complaint about sex education by the pupils (especially the girls)… was that "there was no chance to talk about the feelings" and "they tell us about the danger, never the love and enjoyment"' (p.187).

So, when exploring the issues surrounding sex and relationships education and HIV/AIDS it is essential to consider more than factual knowledge. The spiritual element of relationships, the sense of one's own being and the notion of respect for the self and for others is highly important. Why is it important to keep myself and others safe? How do I show respect to myself and to others? What behaviours show care or love and indicate what I value?

Again, this suggests that sex education, whether delivered by parents and carers, in schools or in other settings, should involve much more than the transmission of knowledge. It should include exploration of the emotions and offer children opportunities to reflect on the nature of love and intimacy. It should provide children with opportunities to reflect on personal values such as forgiveness, sensitivity to others, loyalty, faithfulness, conscience, personal integrity and commitment, especially in the context of relationships and the family (Halstead and Waite 2001). All these need to be addressed in age-appropriate ways.

It is essential that sex and relationships education is integrated within the school curriculum so that it is portrayed in a seamless, rather than a compartmentalized, manner. This is difficult in settings, such as in England, where parents and carers have the right to withdraw their children from lessons. Halstead and Waite (2001) suggest that adults can make a contribution to enriching children's sexual and spiritual values through:

- a greater willingness to respect children and listen to them

- paying more attention to the processes involved in children's learning and development

- reflecting carefully on their own values and on the spiritual and moral example they set to children

- ensuring that children encounter different models of sexuality and spirituality through the curriculum, reflecting the many standpoints that exist

- encouraging children to discuss these areas and to construct their own worldviews.

These points raise the question of the purpose of education. The example of South Africa, already mentioned briefly in Chapter 2, offers some insights to stimulate learning in other places.

Learning from the South African experience

When visiting primary schools in the Richmond area of KwaZulu Natal it was surprising to see the prominence of materials relating to HIV/AIDS in every classroom (Woolley 2007). Those of us working in childcare settings might previously have been involved in addressing challenging issues with children: alcohol and drug misuse, prejudice, stereotypes and bullying. However, we had not necessarily discussed the impact of HIV or the ways in which it is transmitted.

In one classroom in Richmond a whole display area was dedicated to HIV/AIDS. Posters declared 'Use a Condom', 'AIDS Kills', and a list of key messages had been collected by the children on how to tackle child abuse. For these children, aged between nine and eleven years, HIV/AIDS was not only an issue to be faced in their families or community, its implications were a daily part of their classroom environments. It was difficult to judge the possible impact of this constant presence on the lives of the children; it was challenging to see the use of contraception presented in a primary school classroom (Woolley 2007).

The high incidence of HIV/AIDS in South Africa has an impact upon identity and the sense of the value of one's humanity. The constant presence of illness and death heightens the sense of the transience of life, and this can impact on the value that one puts on one's own life. According to the Joint United Nations Programme on HIV/AIDS (UNAIDS 2004), HIV prevalence among South Africans aged 15 to 49 was 21.5 per cent in 2003. This means that 4.3 to 5.9 million people are now living with HIV – the largest number in any single country. It is estimated that around 600 people a day currently die of AIDS-related infections in South Africa (Ruxton 2004) and eleven teachers die of AIDS-related illnesses each day (MacGregor 2005).

This background information, and the classroom experience outlined above, raises important issues for those of us working in quite different contexts. First, it is clear that the children in Richmond were capable of addressing difficult and controversial issues. The question may not be whether children are too innocent to consider such issues, or whether they need to be protected from life's challenges, but whether we as adults seek to protect children in order to protect ourselves. Do we avoid discussing complex issues in order to protect our own sensibilities or hide our lack of knowledge? Hart's (2003) assertion that children, whilst sometimes self-centred, can show great empathy and generosity of spirit (as outlined in Chapter 2) suggests that they are able to understand and care about the challenges faced by others.

Second, HIV/AIDS is not only an issue that requires education about safety or relationships. It is also a part of learning about this world and understanding the situations in which many people find themselves. When exploring a topic based on a distant place, can the lives of others really be appreciated without reference to the impact of HIV/AIDS? Educators and charities often address issues of poverty, malnutrition or lack of water with children; they sometimes form the basis for charity fundraising activities and classroom projects (issues which are explored in Chapter 6). Should medical needs, and the impact of HIV/AIDS on communities, also be addressed? Without such perspectives it is no longer possible to begin to consider the situation faced by many children in the world. The organization Save the Children (undated) suggests that schools can sometimes feel reluctant to talk about HIV, because it is a sexually transmitted disease. But that is ignoring the fact that, worldwide, over 95 per cent of the children who are infected with HIV were infected at birth, not through sexual intercourse. It also fails to consider the issues faced by children whose lives are affected by the impact of HIV within their families, friendship groups and communities.

Third, the statistics show that whilst HIV has affected certain groups more that others, and these vary worldwide, any person can be put in a situation of risk. It is important to avoid the message that HIV only affects certain groups, as this may lead to complacency and risk-taking behaviour by those who do not identify with such groups. This misconception in itself might lead young people to engage in risky behaviours without appreciating the degree of risk involved. Finally, the example from Richmond provides a challenge to consider what difficult or controversial issues are faced by the children in the contexts we encounter. It may be that drug or alcohol misuse, child protection or other issues need to be our priority. Indeed, some excellent programmes already exist to address such issues. However, we need to reflect carefully on how such projects integrate into the wider learning experience of the children and how their delivery (or the lack of provision) impacts on the spirit of the child.

A contrasting experience

In contrast to the situation in South Africa, trainee teachers in the UK are not being equipped to deal with the issues surrounding HIV/AIDS (Harber and Serf, unpublished). This may, in part, be due to the different pattern of HIV infection when compared with South Africa and to the fact that in the UK it has a lower public profile. However, without appropriate education the risk of a rise in the rate of infection, and the perpetuation of misconceptions and stereotypes, will remain. It is therefore important to prepare those engaged with children to face the issues that children will raise: issues of developing healthy relationships, of dealing with loss and grief, and of living a life informed by a positive sense of self-esteem and respect for oneself and for others. Those engaged in health care professions will be better equipped in terms of knowledge about the medical aspects of HIV. However, we all need to consider how to approach issues with children in a way that respects their curiosity, takes into account their age and experience, and allows them to think for themselves.

Addressing HIV with children will be controversial in some quarters and will certainly stimulate some interesting and challenging questions. It is important to have thought through the issues in advance and very important to consider how sensitive questions will be addressed. Whilst it may not be possible to anticipate every issue that will arise, developing strategies to address such situations is key to maintaining a safe, secure and supportive environment for the child. Adults need to feel confident in their approach to the subject and to be clear what they are seeking to achieve with their children.

Most children will have some awareness of HIV, gained through the broadcast and print media. The ways in which fictional characters are portrayed in soap operas and television dramas, and stories presented in newspapers, may already have started to influence their views. In addition, they may have been party to conversations in the home during which their attitudes have been affected by the views of their parents or carers. Some, usually a minority, will have had direct experience of the impact of HIV/AIDS through personal experience within the family setting. The idea that children are innocent and must be protected from controversial issues is difficult to maintain (Erricker 2003), particularly given the influence of the media and the banter of the playground or school yard. In addition, the fear that early sex and relationships education will encourage young people to start exploring their sexuality even earlier appears to be unwarranted (Sandford *et al.* 1998). On the contrary, studies have shown that sex education seems to have a slight delaying effect on the age of first intercourse (Mellanby *et al.* 1995; Wellings *et al.* 1995) and to increase the rate of contraceptive use at first intercourse markedly (Aggleton, Baldo and Slatkin 1993; Greydanus, Pratt and Dannison 1995).

Education about HIV/AIDS may be seen as a logical extension of a school's health education programme. However, there may be practical issues that need to be addressed before any education programme can be put in place. First, consideration needs to be given to teachers' knowledge of HIV/AIDS, their confidence in being able and willing to address issues with parents or children, and their collaborative involvement with a broader range of health and childcare professionals. Second, the range of age-appropriate resources available to teachers needs to be considered. Third, identifying at what stage in a child's schooling issues of HIV/AIDS are introduced and in what context and what detail is very important. Finally, staff need to feel secure in the knowledge that any programme has been considered carefully by the headteacher or principal and school governors or management board, working in collaboration with other staff, and that parents and carers have been fully consulted on the process and are content if it is to be related to a programme of sex and relationships education. It is also essential to ensure that any programme of HIV/AIDS education includes a spiritual dimension; for without a focus on issues surrounding respect for oneself and others the content will lack an appropriate context, lose a sense of personal application and relevance, and become mechanistic and based on factual information.

It is important to consider:

- that the school will not be aware of the HIV status of every child

- that members of staff may engage in risky behaviours, including drug misuse or unprotected sex

- that the partners of members of staff may engage in risky behaviours that are known or unknown to the staff member

- that adults in school may be HIV positive and choose not to disclose this to colleagues, or may not be aware of this themselves (even if the infection occurred many years earlier)

- that children whose immune system is compromised may be affected significantly by the illnesses of other children in their class or school (the risks to them may have a far higher impact than any risk that they might infect another child or an adult in the school)

- whether the school has appropriate non-discriminatory first aid procedures in place.

All these issues will impact upon the abilities of children and adults to engage in discussions about the physical, emotional and spiritual aspects of human relationships.

Consequently it is important to establish clear policies that relate to all situations in the school environment where any member of the school community may be put at risk of infection. It is also important to keep the issues in perspective. Normal activities in the school environment present little or no risk of HIV infection. Indeed, in our experience the most common causes of blood spillage are nose bleeds and cuts on the hands and legs from a fall in the playground. These are usually one-off incidents involving individual children, and so the likelihood of one child's blood coming into contact with another's is extremely slight. Whilst playgrounds are very busy places, and accidents do happen, ensuring that adults are aware of relevant issues can help to minimize any risk: 'With the right responses and the correct hygiene procedures it is unimaginable that a child could be infected by another child' (Mok and Newell 1995, p.266).

We would agree with Mok and Newell in general, but know that it is *imaginable* that the correct procedures and responses are not foolproof. As a result it is important to:

- treat all children as though they are HIV positive (e.g. follow standard first aid procedures in all cases)

- educate children about hygiene and the need to keep wounds clean

- ensure that children are aware of the need to leave hypodermic needles where they find them

- tell children to inform a member of staff if they or another child has an accident – and not to deal with it themselves.

It is also essential to ensure that all teaching and education is underpinned by a sense of respect for the person. Educating children in rules and procedures may be of practical use in the short or medium term, but it is important to include social and spiritual dimensions so that talk of relationships and relatedness is set within a context. It is imperative that these issues are integrated into the learning experience, and relate to the social, moral and cultural development of the children, so that they do not become marginalized as bolt-on elements which bear no relation to real lived experience.

There is no set or prescribed form that HIV education should take, but when considering a health care programme or school curriculum the following points are relevant.

- At what age should provision be made?

- Are there cultural issues to be considered?

- How sexually aware are the children?

- To what risks, if any, are the children exposed?

- How can the children be supported in making decisions?

In concluding this section it is important to note briefly issues surrounding death and dying, which were also explored in Chapters 1 and 3. These issues relate here to children who lose a loved one because of risky behaviours or as a result of HIV/AIDS, or whose classmates have lost a friend. The issue may be complicated where more than one family member is affected and the grief experienced in the school community may be compounded at some future date. This area is beyond the scope of this chapter, but it is important to note the importance of schools and other settings having a policy and procedures in place to support children and families coping with bereavement.

Focusing on families

The spiritual dimension of childhood does not relate solely to children. As is seen repeatedly in this book, the impact of adult attitudes and experiences is very significant.

Families of children with HIV may react in a variety of ways. Depending on how the child became infected with HIV/AIDS, parents and carers may be consumed by a sense of guilt. Parents or carers may have been infected through their own risky behaviours, and may feel guilt that their child or partner is affected. Grandparents may be faced with the possibility that their children or grandchildren will die before they do, and this may mean that they become carers when they themselves are reaching the point of needing care. In addition, parents or carers may need to make arrangements for their children to be looked after by family members, friends or professionals in the event of their death (Honigsbaum 1991).

Secrecy is one protective response to HIV/AIDS. Carers and parents may fear rejection or disapproval from family, friends, neighbours and even medical and education professionals. This may lead them to keep information within the immediate family setting, or to themselves, and result in a great deal of strain as a result of coping in isolation. Families may face financial strains, particularly where there is multiple ill health. Visits to the hospital, childcare problems, special diets and loss of earnings may be some of the results of HIV infection, and these can be multiplied where more than one family member is infected.

Families need to be convinced that services are genuinely open, non-judgemental and accessible. As childcare professionals we are not there to make a judgement, whatever our personal views on peoples' circumstances, behaviour or lifestyle: our role is to support the child in whatever circumstances they are facing and to enable all children to learn and achieve. This requires that we each develop our sense of respect for the others who live around us. Our connection to them is more than the physical or tactile; it is borne out by our shared humanity – which provides a thread that links us beyond any need, illness or issue.

Some recommendations

Ways of addressing the issues surrounding HIV/AIDS with children can involve:

- understanding that blood is a special and personal life force, but that contact with other people's blood can pass on infections and illnesses. We need to take care to maintain our health and theirs. If someone has an accident we need to inform an adult so that the person can be cared for appropriately

- knowing that some people use needles to inject drugs and that this can be safe and necessary for them (e.g. when injecting insulin) or dangerous and illegal. Children need to leave needles (and any items containing blood) where they find them, and inform an adult

- understanding that using words in an unkind way can cause hurt to others and shows that we do not respect them. We need to use words in a kind way. This may help to avoid the use of language surrounding HIV/AIDS and *at-risk* groups as terms of abuse, and help to address stereotypes, prejudice and discrimination.

In addition, we need to consider the following.

- What is the purpose of education about HIV/AIDS in the school or childcare setting? Is the material that we intend to cover appropriate to the age and maturity of the young people? How does it address the spiritual dimension of childhood?

- How will we address any prejudice or inappropriate language encountered in the classroom, on the playground or at the youth club? How does our approach inform and affect a child's sense of respect for themselves and for others?

- How might active learning (drama, quizzes, or games) help to communicate the message of keeping safe and healthy? Can stepping into another's shoes help to develop a sense of empathy and a connectedness to others?

- Does the childcare setting have an inclusive admissions policy with measures to prevent discrimination against children with HIV? What policy is in place to maintain health and safety, and does it include a universal precautions policy (i.e. to treat all children fairly and equally)? How can inclusion and equality nurture the spirit of the child?

- How will we ensure that education to promote respect, self-esteem and safety is more than a 'bolt-on' to the rest of a child's learning?

- What do we need to do to ensure that our knowledge and professional skills are sufficient to address unexpected questions from children? Do we see clear links between spirituality and the development of self-respect that minimizes engagement in risky behaviours?

Conclusion

Childhood is full of risks. Parents, carers and those working with children continually make decisions which impact upon such risks. Where and when can children play, and with whom? What is the level of risk involved in sports or other activities, and is there a risk in being over-cautious? How do decisions about diet affect the health and happiness of a child, and how do rules help them to live safely and develop a sense of responsibility? Childcare is a minefield of decision-making.

Enabling children to develop a sense of risk which is informed by a sense of self is an important part of the spiritual dimension of childhood. The need to understand (literally, 'to stand under or among') (Hart 2003) is a key aspect of this process: 'Spirit is not in the I but between the I and you. It is not like the blood that circulates in you, but like the air in which you breathe' (Martin Buber, cited in Hart 2003, p.67). This air is shared between us all: it means that we can only understand who we are through relationships with others. This necessitates learning from one another (whether we are adults or children) and gaining a sense of the intangible link which connects us. These relationships will be explored in a wider, more global context in Chapter 6. Here, it is important to note the link between the 'I' and the 'you' in terms of keeping one another safe, free from unnecessary risk or harm, and able to sense and feel the self in relation to others.

The concerns raised in this chapter necessitate that a holistic approach is taken to ensure that children are enabled to develop contextualized understandings of difficult and complex issues. This suggests an approach based on an understanding of spirituality which affects the social, political and economic contexts of the world, and all its other dimensions: 'This seems to be an indication why there is a dire need for a holistic approach towards children's spirituality, and one that includes every subject or learning area in an education programme' (Roux 2006, p.160).

This holistic approach needs to run throughout and to go beyond the school-based curriculum. As we argue throughout this book, adults need to nurture and create space for children's sense of awe and wonder, their appreciation of the natural world and their own sense of being unique and special. All parents, carers and childcare professionals have a role in developing the self-esteem of children and in helping them to understand that they are valued and valuable, precious and inimitable.

Encouraging children to be and to stay healthy must be rooted in the notion of self-esteem, for this is the positive way to enable children and young people to take care of themselves and to realize that life is precious. This contrasts with a rules-based approach which imposes safety through prescription. As we are all too aware, rules which are imposed, and not internalized, present a rubric for children and young people to challenge; they learn by testing the rules and exploring the boundaries of what adults claim is acceptable.

Listening to children is an important part of showing them respect, and is a part of enabling them to make their own informed decisions when the need arises. If adults are to help children to develop personal values, underpinned by skills of critical thinking, they need to know and understand the children's existing knowledge, values and attitudes (Halstead 2005). This notion links to the idea of spiritual intelligence, discussed in Chapter 5. Establishing children's existing knowledge is a key part of this process and provides opportunities to address misconceptions and stereotypes. Providing opportunities for children to develop their own views – rather than presenting a set of prescriptions – is more likely to lead to the development of skills that will enable them to remain safe. As Wright (2000, p.132) suggests, this makes it important to help children to consider a range of contrasting viewpoints: 'An appropriate presentation of a controversial issue ought to allow pupils to gain access to a variety of options, enable them to engage critically with the issues, and equip them to take personal responsibility for the choices they make.' It involves enabling children to problem-solve.

This approach will enable children to explore issues of ultimate concern and value. Relationships provide a basis for finding self-identity and a sense of personhood, and for discovering the nature of what is valuable. The ways in which the individual and community interact provide the opportunity for each of us to develop an understanding of spirituality and interconnectedness, and to attain the spiritual wisdom that will inform our approaches to risk. Such approaches are essential in nurturing the spirit of the child.

CHAPTER 5

The Construct of 'Spiritual Intelligence': Is it Really Plausible?

A short vignette:

Timothy, aged four, is in the children's hospital. He has a rare condition called Henoch-Schonlein purpura (HSP). This affects the small blood vessels in the skin, causing them to become inflamed, and body joints to become swollen, while in extreme cases it can affect the intestines and kidneys. It is treatable with steroids, but in most cases, it gets better on its own, and doesn't cause lasting problems. However, in Timothy's case, it seems to be a recurring predicament, and so he has been placed in hospital for a few days. It is evening, and Timothy is drawing. His father is watching him, and begins to ask about what Timothy is drawing. At first, Timothy does not reply. He is lost in concentration. But after a short time, he says that he has drawn two things. The first is a picture of himself in hospital. He shows his father himself in bed, and the other furniture that surrounds him. But it is the second drawing that has captured his father's attention. Timothy has drawn a person who seems to be offering help to a small child in a bed. When asked about it, Timothy replies that the person helping is himself, and that, when he is better, he wants to be able to help other children who are in hospital. Timothy says that he knows what it is like to be sick, and that his own illness has led him to think about how he might use this experience to help others. He says that he is ill for a reason, and that the reason might have something to do with allowing him to think about ways in which he might be able to help others. Timothy's father cannot help but think how his son has been able to find some sense of meaning through this illness. He recalls a phrase he has read about, called 'spiritual intelligence', and wonders whether in fact Timothy has used this to address an issue of meaning in his own life. But, is there really such a thing as 'spiritual intelligence'? Isn't intelligence about being able to solve problems?

The concept of intelligence entails, among its hallmark features, the ability to solve problems, and in recent years, it has been applied to a wide variety of aptitudes. These include emotional intelligence, social intelligence, collective intelligence, and even sexual intelligence. Applying the word 'intelligence' to such concepts seems to raise their prestige and importance, but at the same time there may be a danger of diminishing the status of intelligence itself, according to Mayer (2000).

Along with the above selection of various intelligences, spiritual intelligence is a term which has also acquired a status of its own. It is an expression used by some psychologists, health professionals and educators, and it is a phrase aknowledged by some in the field of neuroscience. It seems to denote a person's ability to draw on the spiritual as a means by which to address and solve problems of meaning in life. But, as Timothy's father asks in the above vignette, is it accurate to describe and conceive of spirituality as a type of intelligence?

In this chapter we explore whether the notion of spiritual intelligence is plausible. We do this first by discussing the notion of spiritual experience as a mechanism for problem-solving – one of the central themes which underlies the concept of intelligence. The chapter also examines some of the neural sites of the human brain that have been found to be active in those who apperceive spiritual experience. It then relates this discussion directly to the world of children, concluding by positing some recommendations in relation to this term for those who work with children and young people.

Spiritual intelligence – a brief overview

A number of writers and researchers argue in favour of conceiving of spirituality as a type of intelligence. Among the more prominent advocates are Zohar and Marshall (2000) who argue for the existence of a third domain of intelligence which both complements and integrates rational intelligence (IQ) and emotional intelligence (EQ). They argue that it is the unifying nature of the spiritual quotient (SQ) that distinguishes it from the emotional and rational quotients of intelligence. They propose that it is spiritual intelligence that is 'our potential for growth and transformation', and which enables 'the evolution of our human potential' (p.13). They outline ten characteristics of highly developed SQ:

- the capacity to be flexible (actively and spontaneously adaptive)
- a high degree of self-awareness
- a capacity to face and use suffering
- a capacity to face and transcend pain
- a quality of being inspired by visions and values
- a reluctance to cause unnecessary harm
- a tendency to see the connections between diverse things (being 'holistic')
- a marked tendency to ask 'why?' or 'what if?' questions and to seek 'fundamental' answers
- being what psychologists call 'field-independent' – possessing a facility for working against convention
- being someone who is responsible for bringing higher vision and value to others, in other words, a person who inspires others (servant leader) (pp.15–16).

It is not difficult to recall instances in which even very young children have displayed many of these types of characteristics. The literature on children's spirituality abounds with examples, and in some instances, these have been directly linked with their spiritual intelligence (for example, Hyde and Adams 2007). Indeed, Timothy in the vignette at the beginning of this chapter could be understood to display a high degree of self-awareness, and to be showing a capacity to face and use his suffering.

Another who has argued in favour of spiritual intelligence is American psychologist Robert Emmons, who has drawn on Howard Gardner's multiple intelligences (MI) theory. Gardner (1983) had proposed a case for the plurality of the intellect, identifying initially seven different intelligences which operated so as to assist people to solve problems. While cautioning that perceiving spirituality as a type of intelligence does not imply that spirituality can be reduced to little more than problem-solving, Emmons (1999) argues nonetheless that spirituality does meet each of Gardner's criteria for intelligence. In drawing also on discourse arising from theories of motivation and personality, Emmons argues that the adaptive processing of spiritual information by individuals is a component of intelligence. From this, Emmons identified five possible components which might comprise spiritual intelligence:

- the capacity to transcend the physical and the material

- the ability to experience heightened states of consciousness
- the ability to sanctify everyday experience
- the ability to utilize spiritual resources to solve problems
- the capacity to be virtuous.

Again, it is possible to recall instances in which children have displayed some of these same characteristics. Some of these were described in Chapters 1 and 3 of this book. However, the question as to whether any of this renders spirituality as a type of intelligence remains unanswered. Timothy could be understood to be displaying the capacity to be virtuous, and possibly the ability to use spiritual resources to solve problems.

Another view of spiritual intelligence is offered by Sinetar (2000), who describes spiritual intelligence as inspired thought which animates people of all ages and in all kinds of situations. She notes that in children it can be signalled particularly in their actions to explore and to cultivate their own innate gifts and creative energies. That is, their introspective abilities shape their outward expressions. Sinetar uses the term 'early awakeners' for young children who show signs of a developed spiritual intelligence. She goes on to outline a series of qualities which are displayed in early awakeners. These include:

- acute self-awareness, intuition, the 'I am' power (a built-in sense of authority)
- broad worldview (the ability to see self and others as interrelated)
- moral elevation, strong opinion (the ability to live by one's convictions)
- a tendency to experience delight (aesthetic preference)
- an understanding of where one is headed (a sense of destiny)
- 'unappeasable hunger' for selected interests (promoting solitary pursuits)
- fresh, 'weird' notions (such that we might ask, 'Where did you get that idea?')
- pragmatic, efficient perceptions of reality (which often, but not always, produce healthy choices and practical results).

Of relevance also, as Sinetar notes, is that spiritually intelligent children tend to be lively, vibrant and creative children who can tire adults out with their focused energy. Their strong zeal for independence should not be viewed as a sign of rebellion or disruptiveness. According to Sinetar, these children are not deliberately trying the patience of adults. Rather it is their 'seeking of unity that is spiritual' (*ibid.* p.10).

Of particular interest also is that each of these perspectives on spiritual intelligence has some commonalities, particularly in that they highlight the relational dimension of a person's life – to self, to other in community, to other in the non-human world, and for many, to a transcendent other. A person's relationship to self may entail knowing the 'inner self', that is, who one really is, or being comfortable with one's self, or being accepting of self. A person's relationship with other in community may entail a sense of caring, empathy and compassion for other people. Relationship with a transcendent other could involve an awareness of mystery, a sense of being a part of something greater, and perhaps an awareness of a life force, or ultimate ground of being, which many have named 'God'.

In the work of Zohar and Marshall, and Emmons in particular, the ability to solve problems is a key component in the notion of intelligence. Specifically, it is the ability to address and solve problems of meaning and value that renders spiritual intelligence a plausible concept for these theorists. Does a child's spirituality function in this particular way? While not overtly using the term 'spirituality', some writers have suggested that religious experience may act as a mechanism for addressing problems of meaning and value in life. This is the focus of the following section of this chapter.

Spiritual experience as a mechanism for problem-solving

It was Harvard psychologist William James who first proposed in his classic work *The Varieties of Religious Experience* (1977, originally published 1902) that personal religion (or spirituality, as most scholars would call it today) may be a means by which a person finds solutions to problems of meaning and value in life.

James's use of the term 'personal religion' to describe the spiritual requires a brief explanation. His interest was not so much in institutional religion, or in the formal religious structures belonging to the world religions. Rather it was in the original psychological experience of the individual, which might lead a person to give expression to her or his experience through the more formal structures of institutional religion. This experience he called 'personal religion'. Today, most writers in the field would describe it as spiritual experience. In essence, then, James considered the spiritual experience of the person to be the primordial religious experience. Institutional religion becomes, then, a secondary phenomenon – a response to the original spiritual experience of the person.

James argued that logic and reason alone could not explain the religious, or spiritual, experience of a person. He maintained that, like all other instinctive impulses or eagerness, religious experience adds to life an enchantment which is not deductible from any logic or reason. It is interesting that British scholar Jack Priestley, writing one hundred years later, notes that while rationality might devise arguments for convictions to which a person has become attached, reason alone cannot explain the foundations of those convictions (Priestley 2001). For this reason, religious, or spiritual, feeling is 'an absolute addition to the Subject's range of life' and gives the person 'a new sphere of power' (James 1977, p.64).

According to James, this new sphere of power enables a person to draw upon her or his spiritual experience as a mechanism for confronting and finding solutions to the difficulties and problems encountered in life. For example, James's outline of the *noetic quality* (*ibid.* p.367) of mystical states attests to this fact. Those who experience such mystical states apperceive them also as states of knowledge which carry with them a sense of lasting authority. That is, they frequently claim that, although emanating from feelings, such states result in absolute intellectual certainty. An individual would claim, then, never to have been more certain of anything in their life, and that from that moment on, their life was changed in some way. And, as Priestley (2001) notes, it is those things of which a person is most convinced, or sure about, that are acted upon in some way. In other words, the spiritual experience may act as a catalyst for living one's life in a particular way.

In *The Varieties of Religious Experience*, James provided numerous accounts in which people who had undergone a spiritual or mystical experience, had gone on to use this as a catalyst for living life in a particular way. This led James to conclude that these many spiritual experiences are valid and hold authority for those who undergo them. The fact that there are varieties cannot be understated. James maintained that no two people apperceive the same religious (spiritual) experience. They are private and individual, and function so as to lead people to act upon them and to seek out solutions to problems of meaning and value in different ways, according to their own life situations.

Another psychologist who suggested that people may draw upon religious (spiritual) experiences in this way was Abraham Maslow. Arguing that religious experience was an appropriate subject for scientific investigation, Maslow coined the phrase 'peak experiences' (1970) to describe these types of religious experiences which may be apperceived. 'Peak' implies a climatic point, hence peak experiences were those that an individual perceived to have changed her or his life in some way. According to Maslow's research, peak experiences may involve visions (possibly, but not necessarily, including religious imagery), a sense of unity, feelings of euphoria and a conviction by those who undergo them that the experience was meant to alter life in some way. Although he claimed that peak experiences are common to all, or almost all people. Maslow, was only too aware that, in Western culture at least, many people suppress such experiences, and do not use them as sources of personal therapy, growth or fulfilment.

And, like William James, Maslow understood these core religious experiences which people apperceive to be the universal centre of every known religious tradition. In other words, Maslow understood institutionalized religion to be a secondary phenomenon – a means by which to communicate the original mystical experience of the individual to all those who also wish to adhere to and practise in a particular religious way.

Other more recent empirical research has affirmed that spiritual experiences are common to many people, even though individuals may not use the word 'spiritual' to describe them. Zohar and Marshall (2000) have found that spiritual experiences, whether explicitly religious in content or otherwise, are quite common occurrences. They have claimed that in Western culture, between 30 and 40 per cent of the population are indicated as having undergone such experiences on at least one occasion. As well as being accompanied by feelings of euphoria and well-being, these types of experiences are said to bring new insights and perspectives to life. Such insights and perspectives, they have argued, may enable people to cope with and to creatively discern solutions to life's problems and difficulties of meaning and value.

American psychologist Tobin Hart reports that his research indicates that up to 80 per cent of participants (mostly adults) claim to have undergone some type of spiritual experience (Hart 2003). Further, his research specifies that between 60 and 90 per cent of them said that experiences of this nature occurred during childhood. Such findings concur with Edward Robinson's earlier British study (1977), which suggested that significant numbers of adults drew upon their childhood spiritual experience in addressing issues of meaning and value in life. That is, those early experiences acted as problem-solving mechanisms for these individuals. While the accounts of their spiritual experiences may have become embellished over time, Robinson argued that it was difficult to ignore the impact of these apperceptions, which in some way generated reflection in those people.

The research of both Hart and Robinson is significant because it suggests that, as discussed in Chapters 1 and 3, children may have capacities and experiences which can be uncommon for many adults. Hart, in particular, maintains that this may be due to the openness of children to such capacities and experiences, as opposed to many adults, who tend to approach the spiritual from a rational perspective. Spirituality exists beyond the rational (Hart 2003; Hyde 2005). All people have these spiritual capacities, although it may be that children are more open to them.

The key point arising from all of this is that people are able to use these types of experiences to solve problems relating to meaning and value in life. This is so regardless of whether the individual is an adult or a child, or is affiliated to a religious tradition. Since the notion of problem-solving is one of the central features of intelligence, this may indicate that spirituality could be conceived of as a form of intelligence. Adding substance to this line of thought are the psychological and neuroscientific studies which have linked spiritual experience to an increase in activity in various neural sites of the human brain. Such research may also shed light upon the plausibility of spiritual intelligence.

The 'God module'

It has been known for some time now that people prone to epileptic seizures in the temporal lobe of the brain present a greater than usual tendency to have what might be described as spiritual experiences (Persinger 1996; Ramachandran and Blakeslee 1998). Epilepsy is known to be associated with high bursts of electrical activity in particular brain areas. Accordingly, the spiritual experiences of temporal lobe epileptic patients have been linked to an increase in temporal lobe activity.

However, the research of Ramachandran and Blakeslee (1998) reports studies that link heightened temporal lobe activity with spiritual experience in non-epileptic people under normal conditions. Through the use of EEG electrodes, they found that when non-epileptic people were presented with religious or spiritual words or topics of conversation, there was considerable increase in their temporal lobe activity – to near that of epileptic patients during seizures. They concluded that the temporal lobes might contain neural machinery specifically concerned with religion, or the spiritual. In other words, religious belief and spirituality might be 'hard-wired' into the brain.

Zohar and Marshall (2000) note that the temporal lobes are linked closely to the limbic system, which is the brain's emotional and memory centre. One part of the limbic system – the hippocampus – is critical in recording experience in memory. When the emotional centre of the brain is stimulated, heightened activity occurs in the temporal lobes, and this can have strong emotional effects. Even though such activity may last only seconds, the hippocampus functions so as to create a strong and lasting emotional influence throughout a person's life. So spiritual experiences, as discussed and attested to by James, Maslow, Robinson and Hart, are often described by those who have them as being life-transforming.

This area of the temporal lobes concerned with religious or spiritual experience has been labelled the 'God spot' or 'God module'. However, it is important to note that, although the God module appears to play an essential biological role in spiritual experience, it neither proves nor disproves the existence of God or whether people can communicate with a divine source. Also, the research described here is controversial. Fontana (2003) argues that this type of study requires extensive replication before it can be concluded that temporal lobe activity is involved in the experiences reported by people across different cultures and throughout the ages, that have been labelled as spiritual. Nonetheless, the research of Persinger and of Ramachandran and Blakeslee does suggest that, from a biological perspective, aspects of the human brain may have evolved which render human beings capable of spirituality.

Association areas of the mind

Other researchers, in particular Andrew Newberg, d'Aquili and Rause (2001), have argued that the temporal lobe and limbic system linked with it are not solely responsible for the complexity and diversity of religious and spiritual experiences. Newberg et al. maintain that there are potentially many other structures involved in the apperception of spiritual experience. They have identified four association areas of the human brain – the visual, the orientation, the attention and the verbal conceptual – which interact to produce the mind's spiritual potential. These four association areas are the most complex neurological compositions in the brain. And, according to Newberg et al., all are required to explain the vast array of spiritual experiences that can be apperceived by people. For instance, they describe how these structures combine and interact during the state of passive meditation to shield the mind from the intrusion of superfluous sensory input, a process known as 'deafferentation' (p.118). In this state, the orientation area is deprived of the information needed to create the spatial context in which the self can be oriented. Since there would be no line of distinction between the self and the rest of the universe, the mind then perceives a neurological reality consistent with many mystical descriptions of ultimate spiritual union. In such a state, the mind exists without ego in a state of pure, undifferentiated awareness.

In discussing the architecture of the brain, Newberg *et al.* maintain that the human brain has evolved over millions of years to address issues of survival and adaptation to the environment. The goal of every living brain, they claim, is to enhance the individual's chances of survival by reacting to sensory data, and translating this into a negotiable reading of the world. In other words, the function of the human brain is to solve problems, one of the central features of intelligence. So, did the structures involved in spiritual experience evolve explicitly for the purpose of enabling people to address problems of meaning and value in life? Perhaps, initially, they did not. But this does not mean that their usefulness for this function was not recognized by the forces of evolution. Newberg and his colleagues argue that although the particular structures involved in spiritual experience developed, in all probability, from simpler neurological processes that evolved to address more basic survival needs, their potential for the spiritual always existed. As evolution proceeded, the prospect for the spiritual and its usefulness in addressing problems of meaning and value was realized and favoured by the process of natural selection. If, then, the human brain has evolved with structures to enable an individual to draw upon spiritual experience in this way, it may indicate that the notion of spiritual intelligence is plausible.

Neural machinery, problem-solving and spiritual intelligence

The idea that the human brain contains structures which enable people to address, and to creatively solve problems of meaning and value in life, strengthens the case for considering spirituality as a type of intelligence, and aligns with the arguments of both Emmons (1999) and Zohar and Marshall (2000). Emmons describes spiritual intelligence as a set of capabilities that enable people to solve problems and attain goals in everyday life. He cites the existence of spiritually exceptional individuals in history, such as Teresa of Avila, John of the Cross, and Sufi master Ibn Al'-Arabi, who serve as evidence that such spiritual capabilities can be highly developed in certain individuals.

Zohar and Marshall describe spiritual intelligence as the mental aptitude used by human beings to address and find solutions to problems of meaning and value, and to place their lives and actions into a wider, richer, meaning-giving context. For Zohar and Marshall, it is not the isolated modules of neural networks that render spiritual intelligence plausible, but rather the inte-grated manner in which these function together. They refer to this as the 'integrating whole-brain phenomena' (p.112) of 40 Hz oscillations. When a person perceives an object, for example a tennis ball, the many neurons involved in that perception oscillate in unison, the frequency of which is around 40 Hz. These oscillations unite the many localized perceptual responses to that tennis ball – its shape, colour, size, and so on. When such 40 Hz oscillations occur across the whole brain they have the capability of bind-ing individual perceptual and cognitive events in the brain into a larger, more meaningful context. According to Zohar and Marshall, these synchronous neural oscillations are the basis for all consciousness itself and for all unified conscious experience. They provide human beings with the ability to frame and reframe experience, and to perceive meaning. These synchronous oscilla-tions in the 40 Hz range are the basis for what Zohar and Marshall have described as the higher-order, unitive or spiritual intelligence.

However, such understandings have not flourished without critique, and scholars such as Fontana (2003) have remained sceptical. Even if the case for spiritual intelligence proves sustainable, Fontana argues that it does not dis-close the evolutionary advantage that it might confer upon the human race. For example, the description of spiritual intelligence offered by Zohar and Marshall seems more concerned with the quality of human life than with the physical survival of the human species. According to Fontana, such descrip-tions are also closely linked with altruism, a problematic concept because it does not necessarily enhance the survival prospects for members of a species. Even if spiritual intelligence is linked with altruism, Fontana suggests that it would be difficult to conceive of it as an attribute that had been selected in the evolution of the human species because it would not necessarily enhance its chances of survival, although in some instances, it could advance the survival of a species by making sure that others survive.

Another who has expressed reservations about the concept of spiritual intelligence is psychologist John Mayer. Although he does not rule out the possibility of its existence, Mayer (2000) contends that the hallmark of intelli-gence is not problem-solving, but rather the capacity to carry out abstract reasoning. Also, for Mayer, the concept of spiritual intelligence is not highly distinguishable from spirituality itself. He suggests that spiritual intelligence could simply be a re-labelling of spirituality. He considers the case of a young child who might be considered spiritual, and who is said to communicate reg-ularly with what might be considered a divine presence. However, whether or not one might consider that child to be spiritually intelligent is irrelevant to that child's conscious experience of spirituality itself.

Spiritual intelligence – a plausible concept

So, where does all of this leave us? The arguments put forward by Fontana and Mayer certainly indicate that caution should be observed in viewing spirituality as a type of intelligence. Yet an exploration of the ideas of individual spiritual experience, neural sites and the architecture of the human brain involved in problem-solving render the concept of spiritual intelligence credible. If the function of the human brain is to solve problems, as Newberg and his colleagues argue, and the spiritual experiences apperceived by people do in fact enable them to address problems of meaning and value in life, then we argue that the notion of spiritual intelligence is plausible.

Given, then, that the concept of spiritual intelligence is credible, it pertains not only to the lives of adults, but also to the world of children and young people. In the concluding section of this chapter, we make some recommendations in relation to spiritual intelligence for those who work with children and young people.

Some recommendations

The following recommendations for recognizing the validity of spiritual intelligence and for helping children to develop their spiritual intelligence are offered broadly. They may be beneficial for parents, teachers, and others who work with or engage with children in various capacities.

- First, if those who work with children and young people wish to use the term 'spiritual intelligence' in their discourse, they need to determine their own usage of this terminology in light of the research that has led to the emergence of this phrase. In other words, there is a need to know and understand that spiritual intelligence pertains to a person – adult or child – addressing and solving issues of meaning and value in life. Spiritual intelligence is not simply a catchy phrase which can have meaning attached to it by anyone and everyone.

- Begin to identify the issues of meaning and value which children confront daily in their lives. These are numerous, and the research of Coles (1990), Hart (2003) and Scott (2004) suggest that children are natural philosophers when it comes to such issues. In other words, matters concerning meaning and value confront children, as they do adults, in their everyday lives, and children do search for meaning in relation to them (Hyde 2008). For example, Berryman (1991) suggests that such issues could include those centred on dying, the need to create personal meaning, a sense of aloneness (despite being in community), and what it means as a human being to experience freedom. While children may experience and speak of these issues in different ways to adults, they are nonetheless real for them, and comprise a part of their world, as other chapters in this book have illustrated.

- Be aware that even very young children can and do apperceive spiritual experiences on which they can draw as a mechanism for addressing problems of meaning and value in life. For some children, these experiences will tune them into the more subtle levels of reality, and may involve them seeing visions, hearing voices, feeling energy, or having the ability to know intuitively things at a distance (see Chapters 1 and 3). Such children in fact experience something of the multidimensional and mysterious nature of the universe. These children will require the support and sensitivity of the adults in their lives, who, as we detailed in Chapters 1 and 3, must assist these children to integrate their experiences and so be nurtured by them. For other children, spiritual experience may take a more seemingly mundane form, and comprise the everyday events of childhood. Both of these types of spiritual experience – the ordinary and the extraordinary – may be drawn upon by children as a means by which to address problems of meaning and value in their daily lives. When children do this, they may be using their spiritual intelligence.

- Zohar and Marshall (2000) indicate that one of the features of highly developed SQ entails a high degree of self-awareness. Activities which involve the arts – particularly music, painting and drama – enable children to develop such self-awareness. No matter what the setting, those who work and spend time with young children need to look for opportunities to engage children in these types of activities. Chapter 2 outlined some examples in relation to this point.

- A highly developed spiritual quotient is also characterized by a marked tendency to ask 'why?' or 'what if?' questions and to seek 'fundamental' answers (Zohar and Marshall 2000). This being the case, adults who work and engage with children need to take these kinds of questions seriously – no matter how annoying they may be! (Yes, at times, such 'pesterings' of children may be extremely irritating.) In asking these types of questions, children are essentially engaging with issues of meaning and value. They are being natural philosophers and are, potentially at least, addressing questions of meaning. By engaging thoughtfully with them in addressing these questions, adults may assist children in further developing their spiritual intelligence.

- As was evidenced by Timothy in the vignette at the beginning of this chapter, children often show a remarkable capacity to face and use suffering, and to transcend pain in their own lives (see also Pridmore and Pridmore 2004). Such pain could include those daily physical and emotional hurts which are common in childhood, as well as those which are more serious in nature and require hospitalization – even those that are terminal. This is an important feature which adults need to recognize in children. It is often their spiritual experience that enables them to face and transcend pain and suffering. For some, illness may even be the spiritual experience.

- Emmons (1999) suggests that the capacity to engage in virtuous behaviour is a characteristic of spiritual intelligence. While children often display virtuous behaviour spontaneously and even naturally, the capacity to be virtuous is one not particularly valued in Western culture. It tends to be suppressed (Hay and Nye 2006), and in some young people appears to be lacking altogether, along with empathy (de Souza 2006). The capacity to display virtuousness, along with empathy, has become a 'skill' that needs to be taught, practised regularly and mastered. Teachers who work in both kindergarten and classroom contexts have an onus placed upon them to build into the curriculum opportunities for children to engage with, practise and master such behaviours. This may be readily achieved in subject areas which incorporate elements of personal development, citizenship and possibly religious education.

- The contemplation of issues of meaning and value requires spaces characterized by silence, stillness and solitude. Yet in contemporary Western culture, these features are frequently absent from the world inhabited by children. Secular and consumer culture tends to fill silences with sound – music, idle chatter, the noise of traffic and the constant hum of the computer, to name but a few examples of intrusive clutter which abounds in daily life. Stillness is usually equated with laziness, and children are encouraged by society generally to fill the stillness with activity of one kind or another. Since children often begin their formal schooling with little experience of silence and stillness, these can again be considered 'skills' which need to be taught and mastered by students if they are to engage with issues of meaning and value, and hence to use spiritual intelligence to address these issues. Therefore, opportunities for children to engage in silence and stillness need to be consciously planned and built into the curriculum by educators. Even young children in kindergartens or in their first year of formal schooling can engage in silence and stillness. Initially, of course, this would be for short periods of time. However, with frequent opportunities for practice, these periods can be gradually increased. Anecdotal evidence from many classroom practitioners suggests beyond doubt that children enjoy such opportunities when they are provided, and do in fact become quite skilled at being still and remaining silent.

Conclusion

The suggestions above are by no means exhaustive. They are intended as start-ing points for discussion and for becoming aware of and helping to develop children's spiritual intelligence. The world of children abounds with problems and issues which may present to them as matters of meaning and value in one way or another. As adults, we have a responsibility to take these concerns seri-ously, and to help and support children in the development of their spiritual intelligence. Being aware of this facet of children's lives may also enable us, as adults, to attend to, and perhaps rekindle and nurture, our own spiritual intelligence.

PART III
Children's Lives

CHAPTER 6

Relatedness: Spirituality and Children's Worldviews

Children are surrounded by global issues. The news media continually present children with complex and often controversial ideas; their spending power (and their influence on the spending of adults) is highly significant and has ethical implications; and the ways in which organizations working with children are managed and run communicates significant messages about behaviour, self-esteem and the values of society. It is important to help children to consider their responses.

An important aspect of spirituality is about sensing how one fits into the world at a range of levels. This chapter presents a challenge to approach global issues in ways that help children to develop their own views and to ensure that issues are tackled with consistency and integrity. It draws upon a variety of settings to consider how an awareness of global issues can be nurtured.

It is important to help children to explore their own self-image, values, relationships and worldviews. They need to consider the impact of their choices and use of resources. This involves a sense of being spiritually connected to others at local, national and international levels, and of sharing a responsibility for the well-being of others. Achieving this is the challenge for the effective development of the skills necessary to become global citizens: it enables children to consider their interrelatedness with other people and with their environment.

A sense of interconnectedness

David was woken by the shouts of his son, Robert, in the middle of the night. Robert was calling out for his mum. He always fell asleep with the hall light on, and could not settle if the room was dark. On this occasion he had woken to total darkness and was scared. His repeated shouts brought his dad to comfort him, and together they looked around so that

Robert could be convinced that there was no one in the room. They checked under the bed and in the cupboard. 'You see,' David said, 'there is no one here.' 'But God is here,' Robert replied. In the setting of a religiously committed family, David could not argue with his son's observation.

The notion of others being present with us, and sometimes of those others being seen or sensed in some way, has been discussed in Chapter 3. In this chapter the link to others is addressed on a more functional and perhaps immediately tangible level: the level of being dependent on and interdependent with others. The others that we rely on are not always seen or sensed: each of us relies heavily on a significant number of people for the resources, services and goods that we use in everyday life. Whether it be the food we eat, the clothes we wear or the quality of our environment, we depend on people from around the world: their industry provides for our needs, and our consumption impacts on their livelihoods. In a very real sense we are never alone; our lives are saturated by the contribution of others to our needs and well-being.

How do we enable children to gain a sense of the way in which we are all dependent on others? There may be no link to such people in terms of a known identity or a direct relationship with them, but there is a physical link in terms of receiving goods or services from them, and there is a more intangible connection, which we argue here is a spiritual link, through interdependence and shared humanity.

Connecting with distant others

The lives of children and young people are increasingly shaped by what happens in other parts of the world. It is important to enable children to gain the knowledge, understanding, skills and values that they need to participate in ensuring their own, and others', well-being, and to make a positive contribution, both locally and globally (Oxfam 2006a, 2006b).

Robert's sense of not being alone, which was described above, may provide one way of understanding the interconnectedness of a global community. His belief in God may lead him to consider how all people are viewed and valued, and to reflect on the experience of others in situations very different from his own; if God is always with him, he may surmise that God is with every person. This perception may affect his worldview and the way in which he appreciates the value of all people and the things they have in common. Others will find such a sense of connection by other routes, as will be outlined later in this chapter.

At odds with a sense of connectedness among people is the knowledge that the current use of the world's resources is inequitable and unsustainable. As the gap between rich and poor widens, poverty continues to deny millions of people around the world their basic rights. Developing a clear worldview is a powerful tool for changing the world by considering connections and inter-dependence among people. It is important to consider how to encourage children and young people to develop empathy with, and an active concern for, those with whom they share this world, and indeed to care for the planet itself.

Developing a sense of being a global citizen encourages children and young people to explore, develop and express their own values and opinions, whilst listening to, and respecting, other people's points of view. This is an important step towards children and young people making informed choices as to how they exercise their own rights and their responsibilities to others (Oxfam 2006a). There are no set answers to guide such choices, but we can support the development of skills and critical thinking to begin to work towards them. We contend that such skills and awareness must extend into the realm of the spiritual, so that the ineffable sense of self and other are addressed in a truly holistic manner. They support the ability to address and solve problems of meaning in life, addressed in Chapter 5 through the notion of spiritual intelligence.

Children as moral agents for change

In the context of developing a sense of global issues, it is essential to consider where and how children access information, how they process it and what impact it has upon them. The idea that children are innocent regarding issues relating to poverty, natural disaster, warfare or terrorist attack in the present day is difficult to sustain. The televised news media show graphic images regularly in each hourly bulletin, and children form a part of the wider audience.

Those of us who were working or living with children and young people at the time of the 11 September 2001 attacks in the United States, or the London bombings of 7 July 2005 in the UK, know all too well the impact that such events have on all children, with and without faith. Many readers will have experienced these or other, similar situations. We observed, and experienced, a wide range of emotions around these times: fear, anger, insecurity, empathy, confusion and uncertainty. On the first of these occasions we observed the reactions of primary school children, and on the second those of high school students. Both groups needed to discuss the situation and to articulate their feelings in order to begin to make sense of what they had seen. They felt emotions which were powerful and difficult to control or explain.

In the context of the events noted above, we encountered children who were aware that a major event had taken place and who needed to try to gain an understanding of its meaning. They were not protected from the news of the events. They were not innocent to the implications of what they heard from the media and members of their own families, and they also reflected on the pictures presented by the news media. Clive Erricker (2003) suggests that the notion of protecting childhood innocence is flawed in some regards. He suggests that children need to develop their capacities to deal effectively with their lived experience and to reflect critically on their contexts. These issues have already been touched upon in Chapter 4.

Erricker suggests that there are two ways of knowing. The first involves being *streetwise* and is linked with a notion of being too worldly at too young an age. The second is, 'the notion of being aware and having developed certain principles and values that you act in accordance with when they are challenged' (p.5). This second kind of knowing provides the grounding needed to underpin an understanding of the different lives of others and the ways in which we relate on a range of levels.

The primary school children wanted to know why the attacks had happened. Might they happen again? Could this happen in our community? The discussions were far from conclusive, and we had to acknowledge that there are many things in this world that are uncertain. However, we also discussed what we could do on a local level, as we felt powerless to make any impact on a global scale. We concluded that our own offerings of friendship, kindness and care might make some small difference to our own small community and that this might bring a sense of hope and security to those we lived amongst. In terms of our own well-being it gave us a sense of being able to make a difference and to have a positive impact on a world that suddenly felt very bleak and insecure. Herein lies the sense of thinking globally, and acting locally: acting on the level where one has some degree of power and influence to work for good.

The children's discussions also indicate the ways in which children feel engagement with the wider world. Whilst the events themselves were far removed from their home settings by hundreds and even thousands of miles, the children felt their impact most immediately. Whilst it can be argued that the distant events 'appeared' in the children's homes, through the broadcast

media, and were in this sense very close to home, there is also an
that distant events provoked feelings of empathy and the opportun
tify with others and be challenged by their plight. This suggests that children
have a sense of connectedness to various others with whom they have no
direct contact. As adults we need to listen carefully to the ways in which children respond to global issues and to acknowledge that sometimes there are no
easy answers in complex circumstances. We can also create the opportunity to
reflect on ideas and to feel the sense of the moment. At times, words are inade-
quate and our feelings are too complex and immediate to express. Allowing
space for silence – and sharing silence together – can help us to gain a sense of
togetherness which brings a sense of security and wholeness in difficult times.
These times also provide the opportunity for adults to model the sharing of
feelings and to acknowledge that they do not have all the answers.

A sense of personal well-being

In our interactions with children we are very aware of the need to promote
human well-being and personal wellness. Readers will regularly be concerned
with the development of the whole person as well as the development of a
critical mind. We need to consider the range of children's experience, including the difficult issues of which they become aware. We need to take into
account their priorities in life, as well as helping them to consider the values of
the society in which they live. Writing in the setting of South Africa, Cornelia
Roux (2006) suggests that 'one can assume that children can then also be critical moral agents in society' (p.157). Their views and their responses to major
events and issues provide a vehicle through which to develop the principles
that will inform key decisions and behaviours. Readers will be aware of children who hold very passionate views about respect, fairness and the positive
treatment of living things. Such attitudes go beyond the realm of reason, logic
or deduction; they have a spiritual aspect.

Whilst children's sense of self and their own inner depths is very important, as we repeatedly explore in this book, it is important to enable them to
develop communal relationships with those around them, with the society in
which they live, the wider world, the natural environment and with their conception of the presence or absence of a cosmic being or power. This needs to
be approached in a manner 'that takes seriously the ultimate issues of the truth
and meaning of the world we have been thrown into, and that is informed,
articulate, literate and above all realistic' (Wright 1996, p.148). The notion of
truth can be prickly. It implies absolutes and can lead to polarized views and

dogmatism. We suggest that finding meaning in the world is best done by engaging with others and learning from different views and experiences: in such a position of engagement, rather than detachment, possibilities arise for the ongoing development of worldviews and principles. Such learning and growth may come through encounters with those in our own communities, but they also come through learning about different cultures, traditions and perceptions.

Cross-cutting cultural encounters

One way of developing a sense of relatedness with others in this world is through the arts. By listening to music, seeing art and artifacts and tasting food from different cultural contexts, children learn to respond to difference. Roux (2006) suggests that important aspects of spirituality include the spirituality of art, of the environment, of language and literature, of music and of science. These aspects contribute to the fulfilment of human nature, '[to] spiritual well-being [and] the wellness of a person' (p. 156), which can help one to make sense of life and one's own life experiences. The importance of the arts and of context and culture are developed further in Chapter 7. Here, it is important to consider the wholeness of the person and the ways in which the arts can help us to make connections with others. One example is the African worldview which does not recognize popular dichotomies between the sacred and the secular, the material and the spiritual (Tutu 1995). In essence this suggests that all life is spiritual, for spirituality cannot be separated out as a separate element from all others. It supports the idea of wholeness and oneness, and the connectedness of all things. It challenges the divisions so often found in Western cultures between faith and reason or mind and body. This will be illustrated particularly effectively by the story of Suzie at the beginning of the next chapter (p.118).

Finding meaning in circumstances

Mallick and Watts (2001) suggest that spirituality is concerned with 'a sense of meaning of life', 'life satisfaction', 'well-being' or 'self-actualization'. It relates to the ways in which people seek meaning in circumstances and situations, not simply through an appreciation of the conditions, attitudes or experiences that exist, 'but through reflective, sensitive, ethereal and transcendental means. It is a willingness to look continuously for meaning and purpose in life' (pp.71–72). This raises questions about why we exist, whether we are happy, what makes us feel fulfilled, and how our actions contribute to the well-being of others. One of the ways in which many members of Western societies find identity is through comparison with others and a competitive ethic.

Competition and cooperation

The way in which adults organize their work with children presents a range of sometimes overt and often subtle messages about what we value. The competitive nature of many activities brings success and failure: it can boost confidence but also crush self-esteem. This has a significant impact on the spirit of the child. Self-interest and competition are seen as being a fundamental part of human nature and everyone is understood to be driven to work by these supposedly basic human instincts.

'What was previously preserved as a secret garden is now given the attributes of a pressurized marketplace' (Clouder 1998, p.45). The secret garden of childhood is a place of imagination, dreams and uninhibited thinking. If adults show by their structures, attitudes and words that what is important is what is measurable – for example, meeting targets and achieving success in tests and examinations – this undermines the value of the unmeasurable. Kay (1996) suggests that an emphasis on *economic* values (business related approaches and procedures) in childcare settings cannot enhance children's spiritual growth. The principles of the market economy undermine values such as cooperation, respect, open-mindedness and affirmation (Voiels 1996). They create divisions between children and undermine notions of harmony and collaboration.

In schools, the curriculum needs to be broad enough to examine the links between ideas and to look beyond the confines of what is immediately apparent. The sense of all people being interconnected and of one's own actions impinging upon the lives of others goes beyond the tangible or measurable and into the realm of human spirituality, in which there is a sense of oneness that is difficult to put into words. Without this overarching sense of a shared humanity it becomes possible to fragment issues and concepts and to focus on specific incidents without considering the relationships between cause and effect (Woolley 2008). The competitive nature of society brings consequences. Whilst there are some healthy aspects to competition, and lack of success can still lead to learning and growth, an unthinking and uninformed drive to succeed can undermine the value of others. If one's drive for wealth, power or possessions undermines the humanity of another person, it is questionable whether one is really experiencing quality living.

Children as consumers

In many societies children are an important and very influential group of consumers. Their choices and preferences can be powerful. They are targeted by advertisers as consumers in their own right, and also as people with great influence over adults and their spending. Their choices lead to the development of cultural capital, the development of a sense of identity and the expression of personal preferences. Such capital can lead to the creation of hierarchies, identifying those who are 'cool' and those who do not possess the most popular or desirable products and logos. Identity may then be created and derived from possessions and may become more about what we have than who we are. By consuming a large share of the world's resources one's behaviour and related attitudes suggest a sense of self-importance and value superior to that attributed to others. Whilst it is not our intention here to inflict a huge sense of guilt on children, or readers, the development of a shared sense of humanity can lead to modified behaviours which collectively begin to impact on the way in which societies work. It is a question of being open to look at things in new ways.

Windows on new perspectives

The experience of learning about the lives of others, of studying a different or distant place, and of experiencing different cultures affords opportunities to experience '…different windows through which a new perspective can be gained on the familiar [and the unfamiliar], where wonder and awe can be seen' (Bottery 2002, p.136). This provides the chance to appreciate how other people are seeking to access the same meanings or truths as oneself, using different pathways. Herein is reflected the importance of the local, as well as the global, in appreciating and understanding the world – for appreciation of the diversity of one's own community or region can be as informative and challenging as appreciation of wider cultural contexts. 'Global' does not necessarily mean 'distant'.

A framework to support such thinking can be based around Watson's (1993) identification of four strands that contribute to an emerging sense of what spirituality is all about:

- inclusiveness, a sense of the unity and interrelatedness of all things
- assurance, concerning the way things are and the reason why we are here
- inspiration, gaining a sense of being channels rather than engines

- the acceptance of mystery, glimpsing a power beyond and other than ourselves.

These areas relate directly to the conception of global citizenship presented so far in this chapter. The four strands reflect the sense of reliance on others, understanding why the world operates in certain ways (and questioning this), realizing that our actions affect others and that our choices can make a difference for good, and understanding that we cannot always understand the workings of the world and that events can be beyond our control and comprehension: we do not have all the answers.

This final point is reflected by Rogers and Hill (2002), who draw upon the work of Bainbridge (2000), Fisher (1999) and Myers and Myers (1999) to suggest that 'Spirituality refers to a quality of being fully human that enables us to transcend or move beyond what is known to what we do not yet fully comprehend' (p.277). This sense of not yet knowing is important. It is essential for adults and children to appreciate *not knowing* as an acceptable way of being: indeed, being aware of the limitations of one's knowledge and understanding is a key part of being open to learn and grow. It is important for children to experience a wide breadth of human thought and experience, 'which may be a source of challenge and enrichment to them throughout life' (Mumford 1979, p.76). This includes an understanding of cultures different to their own. Children need to be enabled to make choices and decisions, to design and develop their own approaches to ideas, and explore questions that go beyond those identified as important by adults, and which enable them to develop their own worldviews and a sense of being a part of humanity in a wider sphere. These notions impact on relationships and also on systems and structures – on the ways in which the world operates. In this sense they are political.

The political dimension of spirituality

Spirituality can be political because it impacts on relationships and views of the world (Myers 1997). Developing a sense of interrelatedness with other people necessitates that we take on a sense of responsibility for their needs and the ways in which our interactions with them affect their experience of life.

The notion of charity and charitable works is commonly found in organizations working with children. A wide range of childcare settings receive regular approaches from nongovernment organizations, asking for permission to visit them to make presentations about their work, and often to leave fundraising materials. Whilst it might be necessary to raise funds for areas affected by disaster, where the prompt delivery of humanitarian aid may alleviate suffering or loss of life, what message does this send to the children and young people involved in such an enterprise? Is it possible that it perpetuates an image of the powerful supporting the powerless, of the relatively affluent supporting the needy? This does nothing to challenge the process or to question why it is that some people in the world have sufficient or a surplus, whilst others go without. Whilst altruism, compassion and generosity are all spiritual values, a belief in the spiritual link among all humanity makes it necessary to ask such challenging questions. Why is it that, as a result of the coincidence of being born in an affluent and powerful country, we are privileged to enjoy a range of benefits and excesses denied to the majority of the world's population? How do we feel about this? And what do our values and beliefs lead us to consider doing as a result?

That we are linked to significant, yet unknown, others across the globe is a fact with a spiritual dimension. It may stem from some form of religious belief (that all humanity was created by a higher being understood as having certain powers and attributes), or it may be the consequence of a common humanity derived from a shared biology. Indeed, it may be a mixture of both, or stem from other values or beliefs. We may believe that all things are embraced within the oneness of all that exists, as was discussed in the introduction to this book. However we view the world, the notion that we should show charity to others may suggest a power relationship that maintains our own position, and indeed that of other people.

Such spiritual questions are essentially political: they relate to the population of the world, its interrelatedness and interdependence. Everyone in the world is dependent on other people, whether close to home or on the other side of the planet for our food and clothing, for the provision of goods and technology, for the quality of the air that we breathe, for the safety of our communities, nations and continents, and for the diversity of rich and dynamic cultural experiences. To make charitable donations to those who support our lifestyles, whose resources we benefit from, obscures the bigger picture: that we benefit from our excessive use of the world's resources, and that we do so at the expense of the quality of life of other people, denying the shared thread of humanity that connects us all.

The problem with threads is that they can easily be broken. Perhaps *thread* is an inappropriate metaphor; humanity is not held together by a thread, but rather woven together as a rich tapestry of experience and opportunity, albeit patchy in places. The question remains: why are some of us able to choose to support others from our relative wealth, whilst others are dependent on aid

and charitable giving? While ever this imperfect situation remains, fundraising and giving may remain essential. However, it is essential to a sense of
relatedness to consider what other possibilities exist, and are available and
desirable.

In addition, some of us will be faced with dilemmas when it comes to
fundraising. When we respond to national television-based appeals, focusing
on raising funds for projects in our own countries and overseas, there may be a
tension because some of the children in our care should be the beneficiaries of
funds, rather than the contributors. However, the sense of supporting others,
or being aware of wider needs and of working together to make a difference,
makes it important to become involved in projects. Involvement brings the
opportunity to develop shared values, to cooperate and to empathize. At
times, the local benefits, in terms of skills and learning, may outweigh the reasons to discuss the wider global and political issues. It can be difficult to
reconcile some of these ideas. Furthermore, the political relates to more than
relationships, it is also concerned with the use and misuse of resources and
care for the natural environment.

Relating to the environment

The spiritual dimension of access to the environment is illustrated in an
account of a visit undertaken by a group of children aged 10 and 11 years (as
told by Woolley 2006):

> Whilst taking a group of Year 6 children on a walk through the Peak
> District in Derbyshire [a National Park in England] one child, Anita, came
> and asked in an excited tone how much it had cost to undertake the walk.
> We were sitting on a vantage point above the Hope Valley, with clear
> views for miles across the open countryside. I replied that it had cost the
> train fare to the local station, that we had hired walking boots, waterproof
> clothing and rucksacks and that we had paid for the ingredients to make
> our sandwiches. 'No,' she replied, 'how much does it cost to be *here*?' I
> told her that we were on a public footpath that anyone could use, and that
> there was no charge for walking to the top of the hill. 'So I could come
> back here one day and it would cost nothing?' she asked. I realized that
> she had gained a sense of the beauty and freedom of the place. Her sense
> of awe at the view and her excitement at the prospect of being able to
> return one day were quite moving. Anita had gained a sense of the
> freedom of the countryside and of the importance of the natural
> environment being available and accessible.

Hay *et al.* (1996, p.62) suggest that 'given that the religious contexts sur-rounding children today are typically much less explicit than in the past, or even absent', researchers need to focus on 'the perceptions, awareness and response of children to those ordinary activities' which can act as signals of transcendence (Berger 1967). In the example above, the experience of walk-ing in the countryside, which many of us would take for granted, provided such an opportunity and raised a question that might otherwise not even have been considered. Having access to places of natural beauty, and being able to gain a sense of being connected to nature, are important in children's growth and learning. They enable them to gain a sense of being part of something greater than themselves, and can provide insights that affect the ways in which they believe resources and the environment should be treated. Once again, all this is achieved through experience rather than the transmission of knowledge.

Some recommendations

- We need to enable children to gain a sense of being connected to, and dependent on, others in places distant from, or different to, their own.

- Childcare professionals need to support an understanding that the choices that we make impact on the lives of unseen others, in an age-appropriate and positive way.

- It is important to consider how appropriate it is to speak of the political element in the spiritual dimension of childhood, and what the implications are for how we listen and respond to children.

- We must avoid stereotyping those in 'distant places' as relying on charitable giving, and question the moral basis of the notion of charity.

- We need to explore experiential methods for supporting a sense of interconnectedness with the natural world and an appreciation of its beauty and value.

Conclusion

We now return to Robert and his sense of never being alone (p.107). It stemmed from a particular religious conception of the world. It could equally have been underpinned by an appreciation of the natural environment and of being a part of nature, or by the understanding that all that we have illustrates our dependence on myriad others across the planet. None of us lives in isolation, and all of us benefit from the talents, skills, efforts and inventiveness of others. In this sense, we are never alone.

The spiritual dimension of childhood is explored in many forms in this book. In this chapter we have considered some political implications, including the ways in which the use of resources and the workings of economic systems in some societies can impact on the lives of people in others. The interdependence of people across the globe essentially evidences the spiritual link between those with very different choices, life chances and lived experiences. Having a sense of being a global citizen is one way of beginning to understand such connections, and works on a range of global, national and local levels.

Children experience the world in many ways: through the seen and the unseen, the tangible and the intangible. They experience a sense of wonder for the intricacies of the planet; they may feel a sense of connectedness to something greater; they dream dreams, have ambitions and aspirations and imagine a range of possibilities. They relate to the wider world around them and begin to develop their own worldviews. In all of this it is essential to acknowledge a spiritual dimension that underpins the interrelatedness so fundamental to life in the twenty-first century.

CHAPTER 7

The Significance of Context for Spirituality: 'Australian Spirituality' as a Case Study

Two short vignettes:

Suzie is seven years old. She lives in Australia. Today, at school, she and her classmates are engaged in a dance activity. As it is a beautiful spring afternoon, the class teacher has taken the children out into the playground. She has prepared some taped music, and as a 'tuning-in' activity she now asks the children simply to move to the music in any way they feel appropriate. The music which has been taped features a didgeridoo, an instrument belonging to the Australian Aborigines. It has a very distinctive sound. Suzie begins to move to the music – slowly at first, but then with increasing speed as the tempo of the music intensifies. Although she says nothing, her body is speaking loudly as it captures the feel of the music. She begins to jump, and as she does, her teacher can see the dust rising from under Suzie's feet. It is as if something is being summoned up from beneath her feet and from within the earth. In fact, the class teacher now notices that all of the children are completely silent, and they all seem to be jumping and stamping their feet upon the ground, summoning the dust to rise from below. It is a very physical activity. It also appears to be a very intense activity.

On the other side of the world, in Dublin, Ireland, Daniel is gazing out of his bedroom window at the night sky. It is a clear evening and the stars and moon are plainly visible. His mother comes in to kiss him goodnight. But she stops silently at the door. She cannot help but notice that Daniel seems to be captivated by the view from his bedroom window. There is a definite sense of wonder present. Daniel notices his mother standing at the door and smiles. 'The stars tell stories, don't they, ma,' says Daniel. 'and I think that God is up there somewhere…in heaven. It must be beau-

118

tiful up there with all those angels. God sends love down on us, I think, like rays of sunlight. It makes us feel at peace...'

Each of these two vignettes portrays something of the spirituality of the two children, yet the spirituality of each is clearly different. You may notice that Suzie's involves silence and active movement, summoning something from beneath. Daniel's, on the other hand, involves gazing at the sky, speaking and possibly a summoning of something from above – like rays of sunlight. Why is it that each of these two expressions is different? And how is it that both expressions may be viewed as spiritual? One possible explanation concerns the context in which these two children find themselves. It is difficult to conceive of spirituality apart from the interrelationship between spiritual constructs, spiritual expression, language and culture. The expressions and cultures of these two children are quite different. And, although both speak English, their use of language – or the absence of language, as the case may be – is also markedly different. In this chapter we explore the significance of context for spirituality, and we draw on the notion of an 'Australian spirituality' as a case study on this theme.

Expressions of spirituality do not simply arrive in a pre-packaged form. They arise out of the convergence of social, political and philosophical currents at a particular place at a particular time in history. Perhaps even more basically, landscape and geography shape spiritual experience. To illustrate this latter point, Australian scholar David Ranson (2002) recounts his experience while travelling through Italy. He was struck by the contrast between the Perugian landscape of Assisi and the mountainous terrain of south-west Umbria around Norcia, and began to reflect upon how these two locations furnished two different expressions of spirituality in Christian history. Franciscan spirituality, emanating from Assisi with its enchantment in creation, and Benedictine spirituality, emanating from around Norcia, with its focus on pragmatic mysticism, are in part, according to Ranson, products of their respective landscapes. This presents an example of two different physical contexts which, although within relatively close proximity to one another, furnish different pathways to the transcendent.

While any one particular culture could provide the basis for a case study investigating the significance of context for spirituality, 'Australian spirituality' serves as an interesting and perhaps unique example. In a society which is outwardly secular, Australia is in fact a deeply spiritual land, and Australians, like all people, are inherently spiritual. Although it is frequently characterized by silence, and masked, according to Hyde (2008), by a façade of complacency, the inner life of the Australian person is one which yearns for spiritual expression.

Secular Australia

Like many other Western societies, Australia is secular. However, it could be argued that the secularity of Australian society has a somewhat different character to the secular nature of other Western cultures. The Enlightenment and the Cartesian notions of duality – mind and body, religion and state, reason and faith – certainly impacted upon the whole of the Western world. However, the context within which this impact was experienced in Australia was vastly different. For the West generally, the separation of these entities marked a change from the more integrated societies of earlier times when, for example, religion had been a fundamental part of the societal system. But Australian society, as it is known today, began its life at the height of the Enlightenment, and as such it has never really known a time when this duality was not an inherent part of its nature (de Souza 2004). So, while some Western countries are now beginning to strip away the relatively recent layers and rediscover, to some extent, elements of life that incorporate all aspects of being, including the spiritual, Australia tends to shy away from language about spirituality and the metaphysical. This is perhaps one reason why Australia, as distinct from some other Western countries, serves as a unique case study for this chapter.

'Australian spirituality' as a case study

In exploring 'Australian spirituality' as a case study to highlight the significance of context, there are three particular areas, emerging from the academic literature, which need to be explored: a spirituality of silence, a divided national psyche and a spirit of place.

A spirituality of silence

One of the first writers to explore the possible features of an Australian spirituality was Redemptorist priest and theologian Anthony Kelly. He began by noting the immediate difficulty of such a task, since any sense of spirituality among the people of Australia has largely been one of silence, and often an embarrassed silence at that. Popular culture in Australia simply does not speak about spiritual matters, at least not overtly. Most people would not appear to know what the word 'spirituality' means, and those who might have some understanding would be quite unlikely to articulate their spirituality in terms of an intellectual discourse. Matters pertaining to the deeper questions of life and of ultimate meaning tend to be avoided publicly by Australians, whose culture seems to have little patience for those dimensions of life that appear non-evident. Anything which might be ultimately meaningful, it seems, cannot be considered a fitting matter for conversation. To epitomize this aspect of Australian popular culture, Kelly (1990) notes that if the sun is shining brightly in the sky and the barbecue is sizzling away, and 'if the beer is cool and the waves are thumping down there in the surf, moments of metaphysical reflection are necessarily rare!' (p.9).

Or are they? Kelly goes on to note that although a 'spirituality of silence' does seem to permeate Australian life, there may be a depth to this characteristic silence. Inability to articulate the spiritual does not necessarily indicate a lack of depth in the spiritual dimension. There is, perhaps, something about the Australian person that prefers to communicate in silences rather than words. Kelly suggests that Australian people find it difficult to articulate the great mysteries of life. These mysteries are rather encountered in silence. He intimates that for a person to really know such things is to keep a decent reserve, and to hold what is sacred in silence. It blends with the many other silences that surround Australia – 'the haunting silence of the bush, the daunting silence of the desert, the surrounding silence of the sea' (p.15).

In her book which explores the spirituality of teenage boys in Australia, Engebretson (2007) argues along similar lines. Adolescent boys in Australian popular culture are unlikely to use a language of the spiritual to express their feelings and their sense of the sacred. Yet, as Engebretson argues, to assume that the lives of these boys lack a spiritual dimension is a mistake. Indeed, the front cover of her book depicts a group of teenage boys with their surfboards in hand, preparing to enter the water. The expressions on their faces capture the delight of the unspeakable – of the sense of oneness that might be experienced in the very act of surfing, the perception of actually 'being' the waves. These boys would be highly unlikely to emerge from the water and speak about the spirituality experienced in their surfing! But their silence does not mean that it was not experienced. In many ways, their experience is beyond the realm of language. It may be glimpsed in their facial expressions, in their sense of exhilaration, and perhaps in their body language, but not through the spoken word.

Ranson (2002) also argues that the Australian person's silence, or reluctance to speak about the spiritual, does not necessarily indicate an absence of spirituality. It is in their instinctual ability to seek the divine in the ordinariness of life, Ranson argues, that Australians honour the spiritual. They refuse to clothe the spiritual in eloquent words, preferring instead a spiritual sensibility that is quiet – a spirituality that is 'unobtrusive and which remains deeply connected with the ordinariness of life' (p.68). It would be erroneous, according to Ranson, to mistake this reserve for indifference or apathy.

So, in gaining insight into the spiritual dimension of people in Australia, one of the first things to note would be that language, or conversation, does not appear generally to play a key role. If we are going to search for signs of the spiritual among Australian people, it seems we need to look for other clues which may lie beyond language – perhaps in the realm of nonverbal communication. Perhaps this search will lead us to explore not the public outer life, or persona, but rather the private, inner life of Australian people.

A divided national psyche

In following the above line of thought, Kelly (1990) maintains that a major obstacle to any expression of spirituality on the part of the Australian person is the dominance of secular society – the outer persona of the nation. For although Australian culture has come to perceive the need for a transcendent dimension to life, the official establishment of Australia which emanates from the height of the Enlightenment remains one of secularism. According to Kelly, secularism has sought to suppress questions pertaining to the spiritual. In the public arena, the spiritual and the religious have no place. These have been relegated to the private sphere of the individual's existence. In this way, the dominant culture of Australian society has encouraged and maintained the notion of a spirituality of silence. It has consigned the spiritual to the domain of that which remains unspoken amidst people's usual preoccupations, and amidst their 'habitual compromises and strident confrontations' (Kelly 1990, p.16).

Australian scholar David Tacey has explored further this area in great detail and refined Kelly's original notion. In essence, Tacey (2000) posits that the national psyche of Australia is divided between two levels of reality. On the public level, Australia is a contemporary secular society. The political and social life of the country strives to reflect this notion. In fact, Tacey goes so far as to describe this public level as being brazenly secular. This secularity is immediately evident in, for example, the media. Television, radio and the newspapers rarely even hint at aspects of life that might lie beyond the secular. It is also evident in the political and economic relations between Australia and its neighbouring countries. In contrast to the United States of America, which publicly invokes the divine in its nationalistic phrase 'God bless America', or the United Kingdom with its national anthem 'God Save the Queen', Australia remains blatantly secular.

However, privately, in the individual experience of the person, Tacey posits that a spirituality is encountered which is not expressed religiously or intellectually. Rather, it is expressed holistically, in the ordinariness of everyday experiences. This expression of spirituality, of the individual's inner life, exists, despite the nationally projected image of a secular public life that suppresses it. Tacey argues that the inner lives of people will always tend to compensate for the one-sidedness of the dominant consciousness. So, whereas Australian public life is secular and rationalistic, the inner life is spiritual, perhaps even mystical. The inner life will continually strive to embody those aspects that have been repressed by the dominant and governing style.

At this point, Jungian psychology is helpful in exploring this notion of a divided national psyche, particularly the concepts of persona and shadow. As an archetype, persona refers to the outward front or façade – the social self that is presented to the world in order to gain acceptance. In the case of Australia, its persona is one of secularism. The shadow refers to those underprized aspects which socialization has pushed to the background – those features of thought, behaviour and the like that are considered socially unacceptable or suspect within a particular social structure (Helminiak 1996). This does not mean that such aspects are malevolent. Socialization often relegates some of the most unique attributes to the shadow because they challenge the established societal forms. For example, creativity may be consigned to the shadow because it is considered to be a threat, or to undermine the social structure in some way.

The shadow is often considered to be a threat to the persona. The persona does its best to repress the shadow. However, those repressed and perhaps feared aspects which have been relegated to the shadow continually attempt to rise to the surface, demanding to be heard. Their expression challenges the persona. When applying these concepts to an individual, psychologists would say that a healthy personality involves the shadow and the persona playing off against each other. They contribute to a depth and richness of life. However, if there is no balance between the shadow and the persona, and if the latter exerts too much control, it can prevent a person from acting authentically.

Applying this to the divided national psyche of Australia, secularism becomes the persona. It is the public face which Australia displays to the world. The spiritual and perhaps even mystical inner life of the nation becomes relegated to shadow. The shadow represents a constant threat to the persona. That which is repressed and consigned to the shadow continually attempts to surface, demanding to be heard. Tacey (2003) warns that the spiritual cannot be indefinitely repressed and relegated to the shadow. Writing about what he calls 'the rising waters of the spirit' (p.11), Tacey likens the emergence and surfacing of the spiritual to the flooding of a river in a desert landscape. The 'return of the repressed' (p.24) is far from glamorous, and, warns Tacey, as it rises to the surface, it can manifest itself in ways that cannot be contained.

If the inner life is repressed by the dominant story of secularism, then where, if at all, can we glimpse this suppressed level of the Australian psyche? Tacey argues that the inner life and vision most typically finds expression through the arts – through the work of Australian painters, musicians, writers and poets in both high and popular culture who have recognized this spiritual dimension in Australian life. It is through the artistic medium that the repressed bubbles to the surface, often in ways that cannot be contained. According to Tacey, the artists, poets, musicians, painters and writers have acted as prophets, creating works which have in some way reflected the spiritual themes of Australia, thereby enabling the repressed spiritual dimension to surface. For example, the works of Australian poet Les Murray, Australian writers Peter Carey and Tim Winton, as well as cartoonist Michael Leunig, reflect the spiritual themes of Australia in their attempts to delve beyond the dominant secular story of the nation to explore the more contemplative, even mystical elements of Australian life. Similarly the music of artists such as Midnight Oil and Goanna in popular culture have expressed themes which could be termed as spiritual, through lyrics which depict the sacredness of the land, and justice in relation to the indigenous people of Australia.

Therefore, while there exists a spiritual dimension to the lives of Australian people, it may not be immediately evident because the public persona is shaped by the governing story of secularism. In light of this, Tacey suggests that an Australian spirituality is not likely to be expressed through traditional religious language and practices. The secular realm of Australian life has superseded and replaced the religious discourse of the institutional church. It is therefore more likely to be expressed outside of the mainstream religious traditions, and through the ordinary, everyday features that comprise the lives of Australians.

A spirit of place

Tacey goes on to argue that, for Australians, it is the Australian landscape that carries and gives rise to the experience of the sacred. In keeping with the wisdom and traditions of the indigenous people of Australia, Tacey suggests that spirituality is linked closely to the earth. It is a spirit of place that colours all that Australians do. Australia is a country of reversals. It is an upside-down land – a land 'down-under' whose symbol is the tilted Southern Cross. Australia's seasons are the reverse of those experienced in the northern hemisphere, and its view of the constellations is 'upside-down'. Tacey uses the language of allegory to express the experience of spirituality in the Australian land of reversals. While in the northern hemisphere the spirit could be understood to descend from above, in Australia, the spirit is to be found in the earth itself, under people's feet and below the usual level of vision and understanding. He refers to the indigenous people of Australia, the Aborigines, who, in their sacred rituals, dance upon the ground, with the hard movement of their feet upon the earth summoning the spirit to rise from beneath (perhaps this was, in a sense, what Suzie and her friends were doing as they danced, at the beginning of this chapter).

More pragmatically, Tacey goes on to suggest that Australian spirituality is then viewed as being of the earth, grounded in the ordinariness of everyday activity and phenomena, and linked to the physical reality of people's lives. Because this spirituality is non-otherworldly, non-dualistic, and linked to the here-and-now, it is perhaps difficult to imagine. Australians in general are unlikely, then, to articulate their spirituality in formal ways. The Australian experience of the spirit is, as Tacey maintains, existential.

But is it possible for Anglo-European Australians, who originally set out to conquer a new and faraway land in the not so distant past, to experience this spirit of place? Is it possible that they could experience this sense of connectedness to the land in the way the indigenous people of that land experienced it for thousands of years? Tacey believes so. In drawing upon Carl Jung's concept of the collective unconscious and the archetype, Tacey maintains that the deep world of the psyche of Anglo-European Australians is directly influenced by the forces of this new land that surrounds them. Jung himself noted that some Australian Aborigines believed that a person cannot conquer foreign soil, because within it dwell the ancestor spirits who reincarnate themselves in the new-born. There is psychological truth in this notion. As Jung states, 'the foreign land assimilates its conqueror' (Jung, cited in Tacey 1995, p.134).

This notion can be extended, Tacey (1995) argues, to include the idea of the conqueror – Anglo-European Australia – becoming, or taking on the likeness of, those who have been conquered (indigenous Australia). The earth exerts power of the mind, and this can be seen as a direct link between the deep unconscious and the world of nature. Anglo-European Australians have begun to be 'aboriginalized' (*ibid.* p.136) from within. There is, according to Tacey, an indigenous archetype within the collective human psyche. It can take on different expressions and can be activated within the person in various ways. Tacey maintains that the unconscious is already attempting to impose the indigenous soul upon the Anglo-European consciousness. This is evidenced, for example, by the growing numbers of urban Australians who reportedly come into contact with Aboriginal figures in their dreams. These 'big' dream motifs indicate that for many Australians, the indigenous people are the '*significant archetypal others*' (*ibid.* p.135). If dreams and archetypal processes are to be taken seriously, then it could be argued, as Tacey has, that Jung was accurate in his contention that the white psyche is being aboriginalized from within.

The Jungian psychology applied by Tacey here is fascinating, and of course quite complex. But its does serve to illustrate that Anglo-European Australians can and do feel a sense of connection to the land that they now call 'home'. It shows that they can experience Australia as a spirit of place in which their spirituality is grounded in the ordinariness of everyday activity and phenomena, and linked to the physical reality of their lives. Kelly summarized this growing awareness of connectedness to the Australian landscape quite succinctly in noting that the land is 'our place; the place where our lives are earthed and grounded. We are coming to reverence it as our own "holy land"' (Kelly 1990, p.103).

Making connections

Having explored three particular areas, emerging from the literature, which might characterize an 'Australian spirituality', we now make some connections between each of these areas and the two vignettes at the beginning of this chapter, in particular the one featuring Suzie and her friends in Australia. In this way, we hope to illustrate the significance of context for children's spirituality.

Perhaps the first thing to note is that, unlike Daniel from Ireland who uses a plethora of words to give expression to his spirituality, Suzie says absolutely nothing. Hers is literally a spirituality of silence. She does not have the type of language needed to give voice to her spirituality, and in all probability, she would not refer to what she was doing as spiritual. Therefore, any insight into her spirituality, and that of her classmates, is glimpsed through her nonverbal communication system. To mistake her silence for indifference or apathy would be erroneous. Yet, unless we as adults are alert to this, we will miss the clues that may provide us with insight into her possible expression of the spiritual. To the unsuspecting adult, it may appear that Suzie is simply dancing in a spontaneous way, or following the instruction given by her class teacher. To the unsuspecting adult, it may appear that Suzie is *only* engaged in an ordinary, everyday activity – nothing spiritual in that...or is there? You will remember that in Chapters 1 and 3 we discussed the various ways in which children might express their spirituality, and that many of these ways involve what may appear as the mundane and ordinary activities of childhood. For a child growing up in the Australian context, words are unlikely to feature in the way she expresses her spirituality. It will consist rather of that which remains unspoken and deeply connected with the ordinariness of life.

Following on from this, it is in Suzie's individual experience that her spirituality may be encountered. This is not expressed religiously or intellectually, but holistically, in the ordinariness of everyday experiences. In this particular instance, the experience took the form of a dance activity in the playground at school. This reflects something of the divided national psyche of Australia. Outwardly, Suzie is as secular as every other child in her class. Like most other Australians, she is probably not religious. No doubt, she and her classmates enjoy all of the other trimmings of secular culture, including materialism, consumerism, and the confidence of a relatively affluent society. However, through the dance activity it is possible to glimpse something of her inner life which strives to embody those aspects that have been repressed by the secular public life of Australian culture. Again, in order to capture glimpses of her inner life, we as adults need to know to look beyond the secular façade that dominates the society in which Suzie lives.

The secular façade which tends to prevail in Australia can also lead to an outward showing of complacency on those rare occasions in which spiritual matters are raised in discussion. This is particularly true among children. Although there may be instances in which children do in fact want to give voice to what we might term their spirituality, for example, by talking about those things that really matter to them, the secular nature of the place in which they find themselves effectively represses the spiritual, and leads them to trivialize by making light of issues of meaning and value (see Hyde 2006).

Again, this can be seen as an example of the secular persona of Australia consigning or repressing the spiritual to the shadow.

For Suzie and her classmates, spirituality is linked closely to the earth. The landscape and geography have shaped the spirituality of these children. These render it a spirit of place. In contrast to Daniel in Ireland, who, allegorically speaking, experiences the spirit descending from the sky, Suzie and her classmates experience the spirit as rising from beneath them. It rises from the earth itself, from below their ordinary level of vision and understanding. The movement of their feet upon the ground, causing the dust to rise, is in a way symbolic of this phenomenon. They are literally dancing the spirit into being, so to speak, as the indigenous people of Australia have done for thousands of years before them. In this sense (drawing on Jungian psychology), Suzie and her friends may be in the process of becoming 'aboriginalized'. The land is beginning to assimilate those who live there.

Again, speaking allegorically, Daniel from Ireland experiences the spirit's descent from on high largely as a peaceful and calming event, about which he is able to articulate. However, Suzie and her friends experience it as something both energetic and energizing. It involves movement and expression, and, as well as being anything but peaceful, it is unable to be captured in words. However, their bodies speak loudly and boldly of their spirituality. The bodies of these children attest to their potential experience of the spiritual.

Suzie and her friends experience the spiritual as grounded in the ordinariness of the everyday activities of childhood – like dancing – and linked to the physical reality of their lives. Their spirituality is not associated with religion or traditional religious discourse. Yet it would be a mistake to believe that the absence of these meant that their experience was not in some way spiritual.

Some recommendations

In the light of what has been presented in this chapter, we offer the following recommendations for parents and professionals who work and engage with children in terms of considering context in approaching the spirituality of childhood:

- Be aware of the context in which children are located. As can be seen from this chapter, context does influence expressions of the spiritual. Further, 'context' does not necessarily imply continents thousands of miles apart. It may relate to circumstances, social or cultural backgrounds and environments which, although different, may not be physically separated by great distance. In the primary school, for example, the diversity of children's backgrounds within any one classroom may be reflected in different expressions of the spiritual. Imagine, for example, Daniel and Suzie in the same classroom. Their expressions of spirituality would be markedly different. Both would be real and both would be valid, yet we would need to be aware of how the different contexts from which these two children come could impact upon their expression of their spirituality.

- Become aware of children's nonverbal communication, and of how context may affect this. For many children, their spirituality may not be furnished with language. Yet to presume their lack of spoken words was somehow indicative of their spiritual indifference would be a mistake. Other features, such as body language, facial expressions, movement, and silence can be indicators of the spiritual, if we as adults are alert to the signs and know what to look for. Writers like Berryman (2001) and Hyde (2008) have discussed and brought to the fore this important clue to children's expression of their spirituality.

- Become aware of the types of language children may use to express their spirituality. In any secular society, traditional religious language may be much less explicit, or even absent, in the types of discourse children use to give voice to their spirituality. Words such as 'God', 'heaven' and 'church' may not necessarily feature in their conversation. There are, however, other types of language and discourse that children do employ to express their spirituality. Hay and Nye (2006) refer to this as 'implicit spiritual discourse'. This refers to language used by children which, although devoid of religious terminology, nonetheless expresses profound and philosophical reflection which may concern ultimate meaning and value.

- Be aware that in many Western societies, the secular persona relegates the spiritual to the shadow, and that children living in those societies will also succumb to this reality. Therefore it is important that adults who engage with children are alert to instances when the spiritual may be surfacing and demanding to be heard – a challenge, given that such a rising will probably not involve religious language, or indeed any language at all. Where appropriate, parents and those who work with children also need to provide opportunities for the shadow (the spiritual) to emerge and to challenge the persona – for example, by encouraging children to discuss issues of meaning and value when they emerge naturally in conversation.

• Be aware that artistic media, such as painting, drama, dance, mime and music, may provide avenues for children through which the spiritual may be expressed. These media may involve language, but often they will not. They do, however, enable children to express their spirituality through the ordinary, everyday activities of childhood.

• Depending upon the context, opportunities for quiet reflection and contemplation may enable children to consider and express the spiritual. Certainly for Daniel, at the beginning of this chapter, such opportunities would be necessary. However, in a world full of busyness and activity, especially in the West, occasions for silence and contemplation are also necessary. Because such opportunities do not involve language, they may be appropriate for children in a wide variety of contexts.

• Be aware of the ways in which a 'spirit of place' may impact upon a child's spirituality. In Australia, the spirit of place renders spirituality below a person's ordinary level of perception. However, other contexts may render a different perception of the spiritual, and this will certainly influence the way it is expressed, and the way in which it might be nurtured.

Conclusion

This chapter has highlighted the significance of context as a necessary consideration in the spiritual dimension of childhood. The many and varied ways in which children express their spirituality is to a large extent dependent upon the context in which they find themselves, or the context from which they come. For adults, to be aware of context is to be better able to recognize children's expressions of spirituality and nurture them appropriately.

CHAPTER 8

Unforgettable Dreams: The Impact of Spiritual Dreams upon Children's Lives

During sleep, we enter into worlds which seem to be a composite of disparate parts of our lives – memories from the recent and distant past, familiar and unfamiliar faces, houses and landscapes not seen before, or different places combined. For the most part, we can account for what we dreamt about: perhaps it was an anxiety dream stemming from worries about an event at work; perhaps it was a consequence of a film we watched; perhaps it was in part related to a conversation with a friend which took place earlier in the day. Occasionally, however, a dream's content is inexplicable, its vividness unusually vibrant, or its emotional impact overwhelming. These are the dreams which can make a significant impact on our lives, dreams which the psychoanalyst Carl Jung described as 'big' dreams, those which 'stand out for years like spiritual landmarks, even though they may never be quite understood' (Jung 1946, p.117). As Jung suggested, childhood is one period of life during which big dreams can occur. Often they arise during situations in which the dreamer faces mental or spiritual difficulties (Jung 1933).

In this chapter we explore the realm of children's dreams. After an overview of the science of dreaming and the characteristics of children's dreaming, gleaned from international research, it focuses on significant dreams, detailing those which have been particularly meaningful for children and charting the children's journeys in their own words. Drawing on examples from different cultures, this chapter supports you in reflecting on the potential personal significance of some dreams – dreams which Jung (1948, p.290) described as the 'richest jewel in the treasure house of psychic experience'.

The science of dreams

In the 1950s, a series of experiments in sleep laboratories in the USA identified regularly occurring periods of rapid eye movement (REM) during sleep. Whilst in these phases of sleep, people appeared to be engaged in vivid dreaming (see Aserinsky and Kleitman 1953). Later studies showed that children spend more time in REM sleep than adults, with some estimates as high as 25% of sleep per night (Kelsey 1991; Solms 1999). However, recent research by Solms (1999) and Foulkes (1999) indicates that dreaming also occurs during non-REM sleep (NREM), suggesting that the dream state occupies an even more substantial part of human experience than was previously thought.

Reasons for why people dream have been proposed by researchers in different disciplines, from neuroscience to psychoanalysis, with much still to discover or agree upon. But it is acknowledged that dreams can take different forms, some of which are described here, and that different types of dreams can have different functions. For example, many dreams may help to sort the events of the day, whilst others appear to aid the solving of problems.

The dream life of children

Children's dreams received relatively little attention compared to adults' dreams until the late twentieth century, but research into them has taken both quantitative and qualitative forms. Such studies have elicited data about the typical features of children's dreaming, together with insights into how children understand their own dreams and sometimes find meaning in them.

The content of dreams has been a focus for many quantitative dream researchers. Resnick *et al.* (1994) gathered dream reports from children aged from four to ten years old, using the 'most recent dream' (MRD) method. MRD is a method of gathering data on the last dream that the participant can remember having, and asks participants to write down their recollections on a questionnaire. It was originally devised to gather information about the 'typical' dream content of different populations, which also makes cross-cultural comparisons possible. Within dream research the term 'typical' dream usually denotes one with a theme that a large number of people within a given population report, even if individuals have only experienced it once (Domhoff 1996, p.198). Examples of typical dreams include falling, being chased, flying, being tested or examined, and teeth falling out (Van de Castle 1994).

Resnick *et al.* (1994) reported that the children in their study most frequently cited family members, which totalled 30% of all characters. Similarly, in Punamäki's (1999) work exploring the dream content of children aged from six to fifteen, family members appeared more frequently in girls' dreams than boys', and older children dreamt more of peers than the younger children did. Studies have also shown that boys tend to dream more of males than females, whilst girls dream equally of both sexes (Domhoff 1996; Strauch and Lederbogen 1999).

In dream research, what constitutes a 'character' is not confined to humans, but also includes animals or monsters. Children regularly report animal characters in their dreams. David Foulkes (1999) conducted the largest longitudinal study of children's dreams taken in a sleep laboratory and one of his findings is that young children's dreams contain a higher number of animal characters than those of adults. The number of animals usually decreases with age during childhood (Foulkes 1999; Resnick *et al.* 1994; Van de Castle 1994). A recurring characteristic of the animal is that it is usually the perpetrator of aggression against the child's self-character in the dream (Domhoff 1996; Siegel and Bulkeley 1998).

A key finding about childhood dreaming is that the nightmare is a regular feature, with a variety of studies showing that they usually decrease in frequency in adolescence. Mallon (2002) cites reports of nightmares from children, many of whom encounter them at some stages of their life between the ages of three and sixteen. The highest concentration of nightmares occurs between the ages of four and six (Siegel and Bulkeley 1998). Mallon (2002) also describes the nightmares in her study as having the following themes: fear of separation, fear of being abandoned, being injured and attacked, and what she terms 'shapeshifting' dreams, in which a non-threatening character changes form into a frightening one (p.82).

Big dreams

Amongst these typical dreams – of friends, family, school, flying, animals and nightmares – lies the occasional dream which stands out from the others, often impacting on the spiritual life. Carl Jung (1935) borrowed the term 'big dreams' from the Elgonyi tribes of central Africa, who differentiated between 'big' and ordinary dreams, and Jung subsequently developed the tribes' concept of big dreams further. For Jung, these dreams are characterized by leaving an instinctive feeling of significance in the dreamer. Often, they have a numinous quality (Jung 1936) and one of the key features is that they, unlike the majority of dreams, are often remembered for a lifetime (Jung 1948). Jung also proposed that they could occur during psychologically important circumstances. He defined these as times in which tribes would have seen it necessary to perform religious or magical rites in order to achieve a favourable outcome to a situation (Jung 1939). In the previous chapter we referred to the Jungian archetypal symbols of the shadow and the persona; Jung also proposed that archetypal images, which are repeatedly found in myths and religions worldwide, are often found in big dreams (Adams 2003; Jung 1933).

Since ancient times, people throughout the world have recorded this phenomenon. Historically, big dreams were often linked to religion, with people believing that the gods could bring messages to them in their dreams. In many ancient cultures, dream incubation temples were built, to which people would make pilgrimages. Although the practices involved varied from temple to temple and country to country, common to all was the deliberate intention of asking a god to appear in a dream. The dreamer would have a specific purpose for doing so, often hoping to receive healing or prophetic knowledge from the god(s). On waking, the dreamer might narrate his or her dream to the temple's officials, who would reveal the meaning of it (Bulkeley 1994).

Examples of big dreams from more recent history include that of the scientist Friedrich von Kekule, a professor of chemistry in Belgium in the late 1800s. Kekule, alongside his counterparts, was struggling to identify the structure of the benzene molecule of carbon and hydrogen atoms. Kekule was the first person to discover it, and at a scientific convention in 1890, explained how he had done it. The discovery occurred one afternoon as he fell asleep in his chair and dreamt that atoms were jiggling before his eyes, 'moving in a snakelike and twisting manner…one of the snakes got hold of its own tail and the whole structure was mockingly twisting…' Kekule awoke, realizing that this was the chemical structure – a closed ring, rather than a straight line – with an atom of carbon and hydrogen at each point of a hexagon. This discovery of the 'benzene ring' was a significant breakthrough in chemical understanding (Bulkeley 2000, p.209).

Jung's conceptualization of big dreams is a commonly-used one, given his strong influence in the psychoanalytic tradition. Of course, it is not the only means of describing significant dreams. Alan Siegel and Kelly Bulkeley (1998, p.162), writing in the USA, describe spiritual dreams as those which have a 'felt power' – that is, an 'experiential intensity and vividness'. The authors note that such dreams may have traditionally religious imagery, or none. In another book, and writing in more depth on the topic, Bulkeley (2000) suggests that big dreams are a channel by which sensations, thoughts and intuitions enter people's waking consciousness. They can encourage people to see things in new ways and address realities they may have ignored or forgotten. Some big dreams, he continues, can warn people of dangers to their well-being, alerting them to threats or obstacles to their future growth. Some help people come to terms with death, as we saw with Claire's dream of her deceased friend in Chapter 3 (p.64). They can also motivate people to develop greater spiritual self-awareness, leading them to ask questions about what is real and what is illusion, given the intense nature of many big dreams. For many people, the unusual qualities and content of these dreams lead to the question 'Where do these dreams come from?' (Bulkeley 2000, p.6). Children are no exception to this, and many have interesting responses to their big dream, as we will now discover.

Children's spiritual dreams

As this section progresses, you will recognize familiar themes from this book. First, where possible, the child's voice will be heard as they recount the meaningfulness of their dreams. Second, in some instances, we again see the overlap of religion and spirituality. We begin with dreams which have no explicit religious imagery.

For many children, spiritual dreams have an effect on their thoughts and behaviour, leading them to reflect on an aspect of their own life and at times alter their behaviour accordingly. One such example comes from Joanne, a ten-year-old girl living in Scotland, who had been partly troubled by the number of homeless people on the streets of her home city. In her dream she was playing on the road with her friends. She continues:

> We were playing with the skipping ropes and I was holding one end and all my friends said 'What are you doing?' cos I kept letting go, and I kept on walking cos I saw this big light and all I saw was this big face saying, 'Give money, give money,' and that's when I woke up.

Joanne focused on the words in the dream, which she believed constituted a message about being charitable. She pondered on the experience and the next time she was in the city, she asked her mother if she could give money to people who were begging. Her mother helped Joanne to buy them 'a cup of tea and a biscuit' rather than give them money directly. Her mother feared that giving them money would allow them to buy drugs or alcohol, which Joanne understood. This dream had prompted Joanne to consider benevolent acts and also to perform them, perhaps also displaying her need to feel more connected with people who were less fortunate than herself. (See also our discussion about charitable acts in Chapter 6.)

One type of dream which is often reported by children is the precognitive dream – one which appears to predict events which have not yet happened. For the most part, such dreams are often of minor, trivial events in a child's life (Mallon 2002). These may, for example, predict conversations with family or friends, or play out a scene which later takes place in school. Such dreams would not necessarily be classed as big dreams if they are regular occurrences and predict minor events, but on occasions they can make a significant impact. Sometimes they predict tragic events and so show the darker side of spirituality, which we discussed in Chapter 3. Van de Castle (1994) and Mallon (2002) cite a tragic but verified case from 1966 of a ten-year-old Welsh girl called Eryl Mai Jones, who told her mother that she had dreamt that her school was covered in a black substance. The dream had frightened Eryl Mai and she was worried about going to school, but her mother insisted that she went. Two days later, Eryl Mai and 143 schoolmates died, as her school in Aberfan, Wales, was buried under a landslide of black coal slurry.

For children who dream of tragic events before they occur, the experience can be disturbing. Whilst coincidence can account for some seemingly predictive dreams, there is no scientific explanation to account for those which have been verified as genuine accounts, recorded or reported prior to the event. This leaves the explanation very much open to interpretation – how can our dreams show us what has not yet happened? For some children a search for an answer can result in a link with the supernatural. Mario, a Spanish boy, described a dream as follows:

> I was on this boat. It was large, like the Titanic, with lots of people. The sea was really blue and there was a giant, big fish in the water dancing around it. I was really happy and my mum was there too.

Mario had never been on a boat before, but some months later his mother arranged a surprise holiday for him, which involved travelling on a large ferry. Mario explained,

> I just couldn't believe it. I was standing on the ship, just like in my dream and when I looked into the water I saw this really large fish in the sea like he was dancing with the boat. I knew my dream had come true. Some people say your dreams can come true but I never believed them and now I know they can.

When asked how he thought this was possible, Mario replied, 'I guess there is something bigger than us who has a plan for us and knows what will happen to us. I don't really believe in God so I don't know what I would call it, but it's really clever if it knows all these things we don't!' This dream helped Mario to feel a sense of connection with something greater than himself.

Dreams of flying are also considered a typical dream, being common to people from different cultures. Some of these can be particularly intense, especially if they are not a common feature of an individual's dream life. Bulkeley (2000) records an account by Scott, who, when 14, dreamt that he and some relatives were socializing on a patio on a clear sunny day. He began to feel as if gravity no longer existed, and spread his arms out and began to fly. He flew higher and higher until he came to a point where there was a gold or bronze flute, which played harmonious music. Scott explained that the intensity of the dream lay in the sensation of flying – feeling a power and freedom he had never experienced before in either waking or dream life. In addition, his sense of wonder at the mysteriousness of a predictive dream was also particularly strong.

Children's religious and spiritual dreams

It is not surprising that some big dreams contain explicit religious imagery, given that many children are raised in religious homes. Dreams have also played an important role in many religions throughout the centuries, and are referred to in the scriptures of most world religions, including those of Judaism, Christianity and Islam. In these Abrahamic scriptures, passages are found which detail how God/Allah sends messages to people through dreams. Perhaps the best known dreams from these faiths are those of Joseph/Yusuf, the prisoners and Pharaoh/King, which are common to all three religions (see Genesis 37:6ff and the Koran, sura 12:4ff). The scriptures tell of how God/Allah sent messages to these dreamers, encoded in symbols. When Joseph/Yusuf interpreted the Pharaoh/King's dreams of seven lean cows eating seven fat cows as foretelling seven years of plenty followed by seven years of famine, Pharaoh heeded his advice to store grain during the abundant years. In doing so, according to scripture, the course of history was changed for his people, who might otherwise have perished (Adams 2004).

Some children believe God/Allah still communicates through some dreams, so when such a dream is perceived to have come, it is often treasured as a special one. Again, such dreams often come during times of personal crisis or unhappiness, as David's dream exemplifies. David is the boy living in Scotland, to whom we referred in Chapter 1.

David described the dream as 'a special' dream that showed him what God was able to do (Adams 2003, p.109). For David, then, the dream had a powerful connection with the transcendent – which we have seen is, for some, an element of spirituality.

> Rebecca, a Christian girl living in the UK, recalled a dream that she understood to be a symbolic message that her best friend was going to leave the area, despite having no knowledge that her friend's parents were considering moving. She recalled how in the dream she went back in time and was walking past a house with her friend and her friend's family. She accidentally tripped and fell into the doorway of the house, after which the door closed and she found herself separated from her friend. Rebecca understood this to be a symbolic message that her best friend was going to leave the neighborhood. She believed that God had sent it to warn her that her friend was going to go away for a long time, and that she wouldn't see her for some time. Rebecca explained that 'she was close to me and it would have been quite hurtful if she went and I didn't know about it before.' Rebecca felt that by sending her this message, God was trying to help her, but it did not have the desired effect. On the contrary: 'It actually made it worse cos I knew she was going to go and I kept thinking 'Are you going to go?' and I started thinking about it a lot.' (Adams 2004, p.115).

In waking life, her friend later moved out of the area, thereby fulfilling the prophecy of the dream. Similarly, Abdul, a ten-year-old Muslim boy, explained how his dream, of being on a beach with his friend, left him with a feeling of tranquillity upon waking. He went on to say that prior to the dream he had had an argument with his father that had made him angry, and said that Allah had sent this dream 'to calm me down'. This dream had thus had an immediate, positive effect on his mood and also reaffirmed his religious belief that Allah was close to him, and was aware of what was happening in his life. As we detailed earlier, this sense of connectedness with a transcendent Other can be a feature of spirituality for many people (Bosacki 2001; Fisher 1999; Hyde 2004; Tacey 2003).

Children's and young people's dreams of the divine can have a profound impact on their lives, as Siegel and Bulkeley (1998) illustrate with their account of Ted's dream. Ted, who was interviewed as an adult, recalled a dream about Jesus which he had when he was 16 years old. His parents were Protestant but had not encouraged him to be actively involved in religion, and by adolescence Ted had come to believe that there were many alternative routes to true spirituality, not only Christianity. In his dream, Jesus came to him and said that, 'no one could get to the Father but through him' (p.169).

Ted interpreted the dream to have been a message from Jesus that Christianity was the way forward for him. This dream affected him intensely, influencing a major life decision some years later, to join a seminary.

Children's interpretation of their dreams

One of the key points arising from these children's narratives is that in each case, the children found meaning in their own dreams. It was not that they had spoken to an adult and discussed interpretation with them, but that they independently reflected on their dreams and made meaning from them.

Throughout history, and long before the advent of psychoanalysis, people have interpreted their own dreams or the dreams of others. Often these have involved interpreting symbols, and at other times have involved taking heed of spoken messages heard in dreams (see Adams 2004, 2005). But in most documented cases of people interpreting dreams, the dreamers have been adults. Yet qualitative studies of children's dreams show that some children intuitively find meaning in some of them. For example, when David had an argument with his friend and dreamt of a shining man leaving him and his friend alone on a path, David could have simply considered the dream to be a result of being upset about losing his friend. Instead, however, he reflected upon it and believed the shining figure to be God rather than simply a shining figure. As God then left the scene of the dream, leaving David and his friend to shake hands, David subsequently felt that this symbolized God giving the boys a sense of space away from others in which they could reconcile their differences. Further contemplation of the dream's perceived meaning led David to act and to make friends again.

You may be tempted to place your own analysis on David's dream. You may be thinking that his dream was merely a result of his sadness at losing his friend – a wish fulfilment in the simplest form of Freudian thinking (see Freud 1900;1999). You may be an atheist and believe, therefore, that God cannot appear in dreams, and that David's identification of the shining man as God was a result of his Christian upbringing, which included images of halos around holy figures. However, the essential point to make here is that the dream had meaning for the child. David intuitively found a meaning in it. For him, in his own words, it was a 'special' dream which made him feel connected to God. Whether or not God exists is not of importance in this case – the important fact is that for David the dream was meaningful.

Some counsellors, particularly those working in one-to-one sessions with children in psychoanalytic or psychiatric settings, may explore the children's dreams in the course of the therapy. But for all professionals and parents who are not qualified to do so, it is imperative that they do not attempt to enter into any pseudo-scientific dream analysis. Instead, as with other spiritual experiences, the role is to listen, affirm the meaningfulness of it to the child, but not to impose your own meaning on it unless the child is frightened by it and seeks reassurance.

Societies' ambivalence towards dreams

Western societies appear ambivalent towards dreams in general. At one level, the general public is interested in dreams, evidenced by the publication of books for the mass market stored in the 'mind, body, spirit' sections of bookshops. Conversely, dreams are rarely a topic of serious daily discussion, and dreams impacting upon spiritual life are discussed even less – despite the universal shared experience of 'significant' dreams demonstrated in this chapter. This final section considers the implications of societies' ambivalent attitudes towards significant dreams for both children and adults, beginning with some points for reflection. Can you recall a dream of your own which is more memorable than others? Explore the qualities that made it memorable – did you find meaning in it? Was it particularly intense or vivid? Was there unusual content? Did it have ethereal or numinous qualities? If you have had a big dream, did it occur in childhood and/or at a time of personal difficulty? Did the big dream instigate changes in your subsequent thinking or behaviour? If you have children, or work with them, do they tell you about their dreams? If so, do you explore them with the children? If they don't, why do you think that might be – have you, for example, asked them what they dream about?

The ambivalence towards dreams in Western societies can have profound effects upon people's willingness to discuss dreams in general or significant dreams in particular. A part of this reluctance relates to a negative legacy left by Sigmund Freud's work which he undertook in the early twentieth century. Freud was the pioneer of psychoanalysis, and his seminal work *The Interpretation of Dreams* (1900;1999) brought the subject into the public sphere. However, Freud used dreams in therapy with neurotic patients, and the later editions of his work included an increased focus on sexual imagery in dreams. Such an approach has left damaging traces in the West, albeit subconscious ones for many. However, dream research has moved on considerably since Freud and is now a multidisciplinary topic of study, with both quantitative and qualitative studies being undertaken the world over. Of course, the research findings are not necessarily found in the mass market, particularly given that those books on dreams which are firmly placed there, are often of the 'dream dictionary' variety. These usually offer dream symbols with suggested meanings, and whilst their introductions can provide a background to the knowledge and understanding of dreams, they do not always reflect the substantial body of knowledge available from research. One of the consequences of most people being unaware of recent findings on dreams, is that many people do not engage in conversations about dreams on any serious level in daily discourse, sometimes fearing that by reporting a dream, their listener will be able to gain insights into aspects of their self.

Anthropological studies of non-industrialized cultures further demonstrate how our attitudes towards dreams are largely culture-bound. Two separate studies of communities in Malaysia, amongst the Senoi (Stewart 1951) and the Temiar (Noone and Holman 1972), showed how the adults encouraged children to share their dreams. In the Senoi community, parents asked children each morning to share their dreams, whilst the Temiar adults encouraged children regularly to contribute their dreams in discussions of the adults' own dreams. Clearly, in such villages, children would be likely to view discussing dreams as a normal part of daily life, and concerns about negative responses to their dreams would have been rare.

The situation for children in the West can, however, be quite different. Here, children are often reluctant to share their dreams in the course of daily conversation with friends or family for fear of ridicule or dismissal. One 11-year-old girl we spoke to said that she didn't talk about dreams to her friends because in their eyes it just 'wasn't cool'. When the topic focuses on spiritual or big dreams in particular, the situation is exacerbated. David Hay (1985) found that people, especially males, in the West are often reluctant to share their spiritual experiences. Consequently, children need adults who are prepared to accept that most people occasionally have significant dreams. So what can be done?

As we have already observed with regards to spiritual experiences in general, some children may not wish to share their experience, and so it is important that adults do not put pressure on children to reveal what they may not want to. If, however, you are in a position to initiate discussions with children about dreams, then this can lead to valuable conversations, enriching your relationships further. Siegel and Bulkeley (1998) stress that adults shouldn't place too much emphasis on the spiritual aspects of dreams, for the vast majority are in fact about ordinary, everyday thoughts and events. Dreams which Jung described as 'big' dreams come infrequently over the course of a lifetime. As noted above, such dreams can come at times of personal crisis – at times of a parents' divorce, moving to a new neighbourhood, during puberty, when friends are lost. The dreams may reflect these changes and offer the child insight into how they are feeling, or offer them reassurance of the outcome.

Whilst psychoanalysis suggests that dreams are revealing of the self, an idea which makes many shy away from discussing them, Foulkes (1999) argues that such a view of self-revelation belongs to adults and not to children. Children, suggests Foulkes, are unaware of this perception, and as a result are good subjects for dream research because they are willing to discuss their dreams openly. His argument can be extended from the research setting into daily life, where adults who talk to children about dreams often find that children are open about their experiences. But particularly with regard to dreams, there is a danger that parents can unwittingly impose their expectations of an impressive dream upon the child. When collecting data for his dream research, Foulkes (1999) observed that parents often influenced the children's answers, sometimes insisting that they reported a dream, potentially leading to false positives. Similarly Siegel and Bulkeley (1998) propose that the aim of any such conversation should be to acknowledge the child's felt experience, and not the adult's expectations.

Some recommendations

- As with other spiritual experiences, the key is to be an open-minded listener, who respects the child and their views and accepts that many dreams are meaningful to people.

- As many children make meaning from their dreams, feel free to explore this with them, but do not impose your own views. Big dreams will remain a source of fascination and motivation and may have meaning for the child, but do not pressurize them into finding one.

- As Siegel and Bulkeley (1998) advise, do not be concerned if the children in your care report bizarre, vague or confused dreams. Dream recall varies from person to person, and the 'bizarre' element of dreams is in fact quite normal.

- Be aware of the ambivalence towards dreams in society. Children will probably be sensitive to it, having heard phrases such as 'it's just a dream'. They may need reassurance from you that you will take their dreams seriously.

Conclusion

In exploring the world of big dreams, we have drawn to your attention an aspect of spirituality which is not always well documented. Yet dreams have captured the imagination since ancient times, and will continue to do so, for there will always be those dreams which defy our explanation. For as long as we lack the precise science to account for each and every image which appears in our big dreams, they will remain a source of wonder and inspiration. As these children's accounts illustrate, they can also act as a transformative influence, leading us to reflect on our beliefs and actions and at times modify them on our journey of personal discovery.

Conclusion

Throughout this book we have examined some of the key issues and insights into spirituality and its continual expression in children. We have done this by examining and drawing on interdisciplinary perspectives, including studies in the fields of children's spirituality, psychology, religion, anthropology, neuro-science and theories of education, as well as relevant aspects from our own programmes of research. By way of conclusion we now draw together the various strands which, when woven together, provide a rich tapestry of the spiritual dimension of childhood.

Spirituality is an innate and natural predisposition of humankind. All people are spiritual – and children are of course no exception. Although spirituality in Western society tends to be suppressed by the socio-cultural and political milieu in which people live, it is something that can be seen particularly in children, and it can be nurtured if those who engage and work with children are alert to the issues surrounding it and ways in which it might be expressed.

The spiritual dimension of childhood encompasses many aspects – not just experiences of the deceased, visions and dreams, or a sense of awe and wonder – but also a sense of one's own identity, the search for the self and the political aspects of spirituality.

In this book we have returned repeatedly to the exploration of issues that are sometimes controversial and complex. An important theme has been the interconnectedness of all people (founded on a variety of belief systems and attitudes) and the ways in which human relationships express the value that we place on ourselves and on others. The ways in which people relate to one another reveal the value that is placed upon the self and the other.

Children need to be enabled to develop a sense of self-esteem that underpins the ways in which they treat their own lives: risk-taking behaviours can bring an adrenalin rush and membership of a friendship group or gang, but they also have implications for the value that is placed on life and the ways in which young people feel themselves to be valued. This book has suggested that individuals need to be enabled to develop a sense of the value of life which saturates all relationships: one's self-regard affects not only one's own being but also impinges on relationships with friends, family and the global community.

We have acknowledged that childhood is full of risks. Carers, parents and childcare professionals are constantly evaluating the experiences faced by children. Helping a child to engage with a sense of risk – which can be a source of growth and learning – whilst minimizing the destructive or detrimental impact of risk, is fundamental to developing the spirit of the child. The sense of keeping one another safe and free from harm is an important aspect of the spiritual dimension of childhood. It is an essential part of showing respect to oneself and to others.

The spiritual dimension of childhood has many political aspects. The ways in which children use their power, influence and resources have a range of effects upon others, who are often based in distant places. Developing a sense of being a global citizen enables children and young people to develop awareness of interconnectedness with other people, and to appreciate that there are many seen and unseen ways in which they are related to significant others across the planet. A sense of awe and wonder can assist the appreciation of the beauty of nature, but nature's beauty is often defaced when the world's resources are mismanaged and abused. Beginning to feel a sense of the oneness of humanity is one way in which the shared spirit of humanity can be understood, albeit in a partial and evolving manner.

Whilst we have repeatedly acknowledged that the spiritual dimension of childhood is difficult to define or to measure this by no means reduces its importance. Spiritual intelligence enables children to develop mutual understanding and kindness; to learn of empathy and care. It may be ineffable and ethereal, yet it enables children and young people to gain a sense of self and a voice that helps to build personal identity. Fundamental to this is a sense of *being* rather than *doing*, where children can 'find themselves', rather than having to fulfil a variety of tasks and roles. The key question 'Who am I?' stands in significant opposition to the more common question 'What do I do?' This presents a challenge to all who are involved with children: how do we nurture the spirit of children in ways which value both a sense of self and a sense of interrelatedness, going beyond the pressures of the market, which demand that we measure achievement and attainment in a competitive atmosphere?

One of the main difficulties in nurturing the spirit of the child is that first it has to be recognized. But the process of recognition is a complex one, partly because spirituality is often invisible to the adult eye. As we have shown throughout this book, many spiritual, or potentially spiritual experiences take place in the course of everyday, ordinary events, and as such can easily be missed by adults. It has been our intention, by discussing different ways in which children's spirituality can be expressed, to help make the process of recognition easier.

Another difficulty for adults – or at least a potential frustration – is that some children will choose to hide their spiritual experiences from you and prefer not to discuss them, even if you initiate appropriate conversation. The temptation to elicit spiritual dialogue where there is reluctance on the part of the child should be avoided. Perhaps the child is simply not ready to share, or doubts that they will receive an open and accepting response from you, despite your genuine sincerity. After all, it is natural to share our innermost thoughts, fears and anxieties only with those who we *know* will be empathetic. A person who is likely to dismiss what we say, or give advice we don't want, is usually the last person we open up to. Children are no different, and are quick to acknowledge who will make a good confidant. At times, of course, our self-perception can be different to others' perception of us. In the course of our research, many children have told us that they did not share their experiences with their parents because they feared ridicule or dismissal. How might their parents have reacted to hearing what their children said about them?

Cultural definitions and understandings of spirituality also add many nuances to experience. As the world becomes increasingly globalized and different cultures mix on the streets, in parks and playgrounds, offices and classrooms, different perceptions of spirituality will be thrown into the mix. These may not be explicitly articulated, but the adults in care of children need to be increasingly aware of the different forms of expression that those children may use. Spirituality may be innate and common to all, but cultural factors and beliefs can mould it and its expression in different ways.

Thus, to make the potentially invisible realm of children's spirituality increasingly visible, adults need to become more aware and perhaps more open to the many varied forms it can take – not only in expressions of 'spiritual experiences' such as dreams or encounters with deceased relatives, but also in those other aspects we have talked about, such as the search for identity.

As a reader of this book, it is likely that you have elected to read it because you already have a sincere desire to know more about the spiritual dimension of childhood. If so, it is also probable that you are already alert to spirituality in the different forms it can take. But you may well have friends and colleagues who aren't. The large number of adults who have no desire to engage with spirituality, whether it be their own or children's, has serious implications for children. Children need their spirituality affirmed. Indeed, often they seek that affirmation and have it denied – which can have negative consequences, often driving it yet further into the realms of the invisible.

So how can we affirm children's spirituality? Those of us who have the natural curiosity and intention to nurture children's spirituality are in an ideal position by virtue of having that inherent desire. It can be achieved in a variety of contexts, both in the home and in professional environments. Parents and carers are ideally located to observe and talk with their own children. This can be as simple as asking your children over breakfast what they dreamt about, drawing or painting together, or playing with them in the snow or autumn leaves. The pressures and speed of adult life, of course, can make such moments difficult to find, as the clock ticks, children are slow to get dressed for school, parents are late for work, siblings argue... But making time to share these everyday, potentially special moments, can be invaluable.

Professional contexts in which adults work with children can also provide opportunities for children to express their spirituality and have it affirmed. For those of you who work with the same children regularly, such as teachers and childcarers, you have the benefit of knowing those children well and gaining insights into their lives and personalities in depth. Perhaps you will be able to see their 'signatures', as discussed by Hay and Nye (2006), over time. You may also have the opportunity to incorporate quiet time and creativity into your activities, for example, to draw, listen to music and dance.

Professionals such as health workers, doctors, nurses and counsellors may only work with individual children for short periods of time, but this is no barrier to engaging with the spiritual. Children may still need affirmation through an answer to a question; if children are unwell, their questions may be related to the bigger questions of life, and may be expressed verbally, or perhaps through a drawing that expresses their fears or concerns. Affirmation can take various forms, the appropriateness of which may be determined by the nature of your relationship with the child or the context within which it is expressed. Sometimes a simple smile is enough; sometimes a listening ear is sufficient, and no further comment is needed; sometimes, particularly if the spiritual experience has been of the darker variety described in this book, a more lengthy discussion is required. The benefits of such affirmation are, however, intensely valuable. The most obvious benefit for children may be that their spirituality is nurtured. This would certainly be a positive outcome in a society that is often destructive of people's spirituality, and which time and again seems to relegate the spiritual to the shadow. But the heartening element, as we have shown, is that affirmation of the spiritual dimension of childhood can be undertaken in a wide variety of contexts, ranging from the home through to childcare establishments, the primary school classroom, and the more specialized child provisions such as counselling, psychological and even medical services.

As well, there are immeasurable benefits for adults who engage with children. Key among these is the strengthening of relationships between adults and children – parent and child, teacher and child, counsellor and child, and so forth. Fundamental to the notion of spirituality is the sense of relationship and connectedness a person feels with others. Affirming and attending to the spiritual dimension may be an essential means by which relationships are strengthened and enhanced.

Another benefit for adults might be the opportunity to reclaim, or perhaps to rediscover, their own sense of the spiritual, which may have been lying dormant for some time, and to see the world though children's eyes. In affirming the spiritual dimension adults are invited to engage with their own sense of wonder and awe, their own experiences and apperceptions, some of which may be considered to be spiritual, and with issues related to their own sense of identity and personhood, and their own ultimate and existential questions. The children with whom we engage as adults may enable us to reconnect with the spiritual dimension of our own lives.

But the key to all of this is an awareness on the part of adults to the spiritual dimension of childhood. If the significant adults in the lives of children are alert and sensitive to the various issues in relation to children's spirituality, as we have highlighted in this book, the nurturing of this fascinating part of childhood can enrich the lives of all concerned.

References

Adams, K. (2001) 'God talks to me in my dreams: the occurrence and significance of children's dreams about God.' *International Journal of Children's Spirituality 6*, 1, 99–111.

Adams, K. (2003) 'Children's dreams: an exploration of Jung's concept of big dreams.' *International Journal of Children's Spirituality 8*, 2, 105–114.

Adams, K. (2004) 'Scriptural symbolic dreams: relevant or redundant in the 21st century?' *Sleep and Hypnosis 6*, 3, 111–118.

Adams, K. (2007) 'What lies beyond? Dreams of the afterlife.' *REsource 30*, 23–26.

Adams, K. and Hyde, B. (2008) 'Children's grief dreams and the theory of spiritual intelligence.' *Dreaming*.

Aggleton, P., Baldo, M. and Slutkin, G. (1993) 'Sex education leads to safer behaviour.' *Global AIDS News 4*, 1–20.

Aserinsky, E. and Kleitman, N. (1953) 'Regularly occurring periods of eye motility and concomitant phenomena during sleep.' *Science 118*, 273–274.

Bainbridge, R.M. (2000) 'The spiritual and the intending teacher.' *International Journal of Children's Spirituality 5*, 2, 163–175.

Berger, P. L. (1967) *The Sacred Canopy: Elements of a Sociological Theory of Religion.* Garden City, NY: Doubleday.

Berryman, J. (1985) 'Children's spirituality and religious language.' *British Journal of Religious Education 7*, 3, 120–127.

Berryman, J. (1991) *Godly Play, a Way of Religious Education.* San Francisco: Harper.

Berryman, J. (2001) 'The non-verbal nature of spirituality and religious language.' In J. Erricker, C. Ota and C. Erricker (eds) *Spiritual Education. Cultural, Religious and Social Differences, New Perspectives for the 21st Century.* Brighton, UK: Sussex Academic.

Bible, Revised Standard Version (1973) London: Collins.

Billington, R. (1997) *Understanding Eastern Philosophy.* London: Routledge.

Bosacki, S. (2001) 'Theory of mind or theory of the soul? The tole of spirituality in children's understanding of minds and emotions.' In J. Erricker, C. Ota and C. Erricker (eds) *Spiritual Education. Cultural, Religious and Social Differences, New Perspectives for the 21st Century.* Brighton, UK: Sussex Academic.

Bottery, M. (2002) 'Globalization, spirituality and the management of education.' *International Journal of Children's Spirituality 7*, 2, 131–142.

Boyer, P. (1994) 'Cognitive constraints on cultural representations: Natural ontologies and religious ideas.' In L. Hirschfeld and S. Gelman (eds) *Mapping the Mind Domain Specificity in Cognition and Culture.* Cambridge: Cambridge University Press.

Bruce, S. (1995) *Religion in Modern Britain*. Oxford: Oxford University Press.

Bulkeley, K. (1994) *The Wilderness of Dreams: Exploring the Religious Meanings of Dreams in Modern Western Culture*. Albany: State University of New York Press.

Bulkeley, K. (2000) *Transforming Dreams*. New York: John Wiley and Sons.

Carey, S. and Spelke, E. (1994) 'Domain specific knowledge and conceptual change.' In L. Hirschfeld and S. Gelman (eds) *Mapping the Mind Domain Specificity in Cognition and Culture*. Cambridge: Cambridge University Press.

Castelli, M. and Trevathan, A. (2005) 'The English public space: developing spirituality in English Muslim schools.' *International Journal of Children's Spirituality 10*, 2, 123–131.

Champagne, E. (2001) 'Listening to…listening for…: A theological reflection on spirituality in early childhood.' In J. Erricker, C. Ota and C. Erricker (eds) *Spiritual Education. Cultural, Religious and Social Differences, New Perspectives for the 21st Century*. Brighton: Sussex Academic.

Clouder, C. (1998) 'The spiritual dimension and autonomy.' *International Journal of Children's Spirituality 3*, 1, 43–49.

Coles, R. (1990) *The Spiritual Life of Children*. London: HarperCollins.

Cosmides, L. and Tooby, J. (1994) 'Origins of domain specificity: The evolution of functional organization.' In L. Hirschfeld and S. Gelman (eds) *Mapping the Mind Domain Specificity in Cognition and Culture*. Cambridge: Cambridge University Press.

Dawkins, R. (2006) *The God Delusion*. London: Transworld.

Dean, J. (2000) *Improving Children's Learning: Effective Teaching in the Primary School*. London: Routledge.

Department for Education (DfE) (1994) *Education Act 1993: Sex Education in Schools, Circular 5/94*. London: HMSO.

Department for Education and Employment (DfEE) (2000) *Sex and Relationship Education Guidance, Circular 0116/2000*. London: DfEE.

Department for Education and Skills (DfES) (2005) *Youth Matters*. London: HMSO.

Department of Education and Science (DES) (1987) *Circular 11/87: Sex Education at School*. London: HMSO.

de Souza, M. (2004, July) 'Teaching for connectedness and meaning: The role of spirituality in the learning process.' A paper presented at the International Seminar for Religious Education and Values, Philadelphia, USA.

de Souza, M. (2005) 'Engaging the mind, heart and soul of the student in religious education: Teaching for meaning and connection.' *Journal of Religious Education 53*, 4, 40–47.

de Souza, M. (2006) 'Rediscovering the spiritual dimension in education: promoting a sense of self and place, meaning and purpose in learning.' In M. de Souza, K. Engebretson, G. Durka, R. Jackson and A. McGrady (eds) *International Handbook of the Religious, Moral and Spiritual Dimensions in Education*. AA Dordrecht, The Netherlands: Springer.

Domhoff, W.G. (1996) *Finding Meaning in Dreams: A Quantitative Approach*. New York: Plenum Press.

Draycott, P. and Blaylock, B. (no date) 'Life After Death?' In L. Blaylock (ed.), *Listening to Young People in Secondary Religious Education*. Derby: RE Today Publishing.

Durham, W. (1991) *Co-evolution, Genes, Culture and Human Diversity*. Stanford, CA: Stanford University Press.

Elton-Chalcraft, S. (2002) 'Empty Wells: How well are we doing at spiritual well-being?' *International Journal of Children's Spirituality 8*, 2, 151–162.

Emmons, R. (1999) *The Psychology of Ultimate Concerns, Motivation and Spirituality in Personality.* New York: Guilford.

Emmons, R. (2000) 'Is spirituality an intelligence? Motivation, cognition, and the psychology of ultimate concerns.' *The International Journal for the Psychology of Religion 10*, 1, 3–26.

Engebretson, K. (2007) *Connecting: Teenage Boys, Spirituality and Religious Education.* Strathfield, NSW: St. Paul's.

Erricker, C. (2003) 'Against the protection of childhood innocence.' *International Journal of Children's Spirituality 8*, 1, 3–7.

Erricker, C., Erricker, J., Sullivan, D., Ota, C. and Fletcher, M. (1997) *The Education of the Whole Child.* London: Cassell.

Erricker, J. (2001) 'Spirituality and the notion of citizenship in Education.' In J. Erricker, C. Ota and C. Erricker (eds) *Spiritual Education. Cultural, Religious and Social Differences, New Perspectives for the 21st Century.* Brighton, UK: Sussex Academic.

Eurobarometer (2006) *AIDS Prevention: 240/Wave 64.1 and 64.3 – TNS Opinion and Social.* Accessed on 24/09/07 at http://ec.europa.eu/health/ph_publication/eb_aids_en.pdf

Fisher, J. (1999) 'Helps to fostering students' spiritual health.' *International Journal of Children's Spirituality 4*, 29–49.

Foulkes, D. (1999) *Children's Dreaming and the Development of Consciousness.* Cambridge, MA: Harvard University Press.

Fodor, J. (1983) *Modularity of the Mind.* Cambridge, MA: MIT Press.

Fontana, D. (2003) *Psychology, Religion and Spirituality.* Oxford: BPS Blackwell.

Freud, S. (1999) *The Interpretation of Dreams,* ed. J. Crick. Oxford: Oxford University Press. (Original work published 1900.)

Gardner, H. (1983) *Frames of Mind: The Theory of Multiple Intelligences.* New York, NY: Basic Books.

Garfield, P. (1996) 'Dreams in bereavement.' In D. Barrett (ed.) *Trauma and Dreams.* Cambridge: Harvard University Press.

Goertz, K. (2006) 'Writing from the secret annex: The case of Anne Frank.' In E. Goodenough (ed.) *Secret Spaces of Childhood.* Ann Arbor: University of Michigan Press.

Greydanus, D., Pratt, H. and Dannison, L. (1995) 'Sexuality education programs for youth: Current state of affairs and strategies for the future.' *Journal of Sex Education and Therapy 4*, 238–254.

Griffiths, B. (1984) *Christ in India: Essays Towards a Hindu-Christian Dialogue.* Springfield, IL: Templegate.

Halstead, J.M. (2005) 'Teaching about love.' *British Journal of Educational Studies 53*, 3, 290–305.

Halstead, J.M. and Waite, S. (2001) 'Nurturing the spiritual in children's sexual development.' *International Journal of Children's Spirituality 6*, 2, 185–206.

Handley, G. (2005) 'Children's rights to participation.' In T. Waller (ed.) *An Introduction to Early Childhood: A multidisciplinary approach.* London: Paul Chapman.

Harber, C. and Serf, J. (unpublished typescript) 'Teacher Education for a Democratic Society in England and South Africa.'

Hardy, A. (1966) *The Divine Flame, An Essay Towards a Natural History of Religion.* London: Collins.

Hart, T. (2003) *The Secret Spiritual World of Children.* Maui: Inner Ocean.

Hay, D. (1985) 'Suspicion of the spiritual: Teaching religion in a world of secular experience.' *British Journal of Religious Education 7,* 3, 40–147.

Hay, D. and Nye, R. (2006) *The Spirit of the Child* (revised edition). London: Jessica Kingsley Publishers.

Helminiak, D. (1996) *The Human Core of Spirituality Mind as Psyche and Spirit.* Albany, NY: State University of New York Press.

Hirschfeld, L. and Gelman, S. (1994) 'Towards a topography of mind: An introduction to domain specificity.' In L. Hirschfeld and S. Gelman (eds) *Mapping the Mind, Domain Specificity in Cognition and Culture.* Cambridge: Cambridge University Press.

Honigsbaum, N. (1991) *HIV, AIDS and Children: A Cause for Concern.* London: National Children's Bureau.

Hyde, B. (2004) 'The plausibility of spiritual intelligence: Spiritual experience, problem solving, and neural sites.' *International Journal of Children's Spirituality 9,* 1, 39–52.

Hyde, B. (2005) 'Beyond logic – entering the realm of mystery: Hermeneutic phenomenology as a tool for reflecting on children's spirituality.' *International Journal of Children's Spirituality 10,* 1, 31–44.

Hyde, B. (2006) 'You can't buy love': Trivializing and the challenge for religious education. *Journal of Beliefs and Values 27,* 2, 165–176.

Hyde, B. (2008) *Children and Spirituality. Searching for Meaning and Connectedness.* London: Jessica Kingsley Publishers.

Hyde, B. and Adams, K. (2007) 'From biblical dreams to children's dreams: A challenge for religious educators in Catholic schools.' *Journal of Religious Education 55,* 4, 38–42.

James, W. (1977) *The Varieties of Religious Experience A Study in Human Nature.* London: Fountain Books. (Original work published 1902.)

Jung, C.G. (1933) *The Collected Works of C. G. Jung, 10.* London: Routledge.

Jung, C.G. (1935) *The Collected Works of C. G. Jung, 7.* London: Routledge.

Jung, C.G. (1936) *The Collected Works of C. G. Jung, 9, 1.* London: Routledge.

Jung, C.G. (1939) *The Collected Works of C. G. Jung, 3.* London: Routledge.

Jung, C.G. (1946) *The Collected Works of C. G. Jung, 17.* London: Routledge.

Jung, C.G. (1948) *The Collected Works of C. G. Jung, 8.* London: Routledge.

Kay, W. (1996) 'Fowler, spirituality and values in church schools.' *International Journal of Children's Spirituality 1,* 1, 17–22.

Kehily, M.J. and Swann, J. (eds) (2003) *Children's Cultural Worlds* (Childhood Series, Book 3). Chichester: John Wiley and Sons with OUP.

Kelly, A. (1990) *A New Imagining. Towards an Australian Spirituality.* Melbourne: Collins Dove.

Kelsey, M. (1991) *God, Dreams and Revelation: A Christian Interpretation of Dreams.* Minneapolis: Augsberg.

Klein, R. (2003) *We Want our Say: Children as Active Participants in Their Education.* Stoke-on-Trent: Trentham Books.

Koran (trans. N.J. Dawood, 1983), Frome and London: Penguin Books.

Lang, P., Best, R. and Lichtenberg A. (eds) (1994) *Caring for Children: International Perspectives on Pastoral Care and PSE.* London: Cassell.

Lealman, B. (1996) 'The whole vision of the child.' In R. Best (ed.) *Education, Spirituality and the Whole Child.* London: Cassell.

Lefrancois, G.R. (1999) *Psychology for Teaching.* Belmont: Wadsworth.

Little, G. (no date) 'Young people's spiritual experience.' In L. Blaylock (ed.), *Listening to Young People in Secondary Religious Education.* Derby: RE Today Publishing.

Mallon, B. (2002) *Dream Time with Children: Learning to Dream, Dreaming to Learn,* London: Jessica Kingsley Publishers.

Mallon, B. (2005) 'Dreams and bereavement.' *Bereavement Care 24,* 43–46.

Maslow, A. (1970) *Religions, Values and Peak Experiences.* New York: The Viking Press.

Mayer, J. (2000) 'Spiritual intelligence or spiritual consciousness?' *The International Journal for the Psychology of Religion 10,* 1, 47–56.

McCreery, E. (1996) 'Talking to children about things spiritual.' In R. Best (ed) *Education, Spirituality and the Whole Child.* London: Cassell.

McGrath, A. (2005) *Dawkins' God: Genes, Memes and the Meaning of Life.* Oxford: Blackwell.

MacGregor, K. (2005) 'Alarm Sounds as AIDS Claims 11 Teachers a Day.' In *Times Education Supplement.* Accessed 24/09/07 at http://www.tes.co.uk/search/story/?story_id=2090757

McLaughlin, T.H. (1996) 'Education of the whole child?' In R. Best (ed.) *Education, Spirituality and the Whole Child.* London: Cassell.

Mallick, J. and Watts, M. (2001) 'Spirituality and drugs education: a study in parent/child communication.' *International Journal of Children's Spirituality 6,* 1, 67–83.

Marshak, D.L. and Litfin, K. (2002) 'Aurobindo Ghose'. In J. Miller and Y. Nakagawa (eds) *Nurturing Our Wholeness: Perspectives on Spirituality in Education.* Rutland, VT: Foundation for Educational Renewal.

Meehan, C. (2002) 'Confusion and competing claims in the spiritual development debate.' *International Journal of Children's Spirituality 7,* 3, 291–308.

Mellanby, A.R., Phelps, F.A., Crichton, N.J. and Tripp, J.H. (1995) 'School sex education: an experimental programme with educational and medical benefit.' *British Medical Journal 311,* 414–17.

Merton, Y. (1956) *The Sign of Jonas.* Garden City, NY: Doubleday Image Books.

Miles, G. and Wright, J. (eds) (2003) *Celebrating Children: Equipping People Working with Children and Young People Living in Difficult Circumstances Around the World.* Carlisle: Paternoster Press.

Mills, M. (2001) 'Pushing it to the max: Interrogating the risky business of being a boy.' In W. Martino and B. Meyenn (eds) *What About the Boys: Issues of Masculinity in Schools.* Buckingham: Open University Press.

Moffett, J. (1994) *The Universal Schoolhouse. Spiritual Awakening through Education.* San Francisco: Jossey-Bass.

Mok, J.Y.Q. and Newell, M.L. (1995) *HIV Infection in Children: A Guide to Practical Management.* Cambridge: Cambridge University Press.

Montgomery, H., Burr, R. and Woodhead. M. (eds) (2003) *Changing Childhoods: Local and Global* (Childhood Series, Book 4). Chichester: John Wiley and Sons with OUP.

Morrell, R. (2005, August) 'Masculinity.' A paper presented at the University of KwaZulu Natal, TIDE~ Study Visit to South Africa.

Mumford, C. (1979) *Young Children and Religion.* Ilkley: Carol Mumford.

Myers, B.K. (1997) *Young Children and Spirituality.* London: Routledge.

Myers, B.K and Myers, M.E. (1999) 'Engaging children's spirit through literature.' *Childhood Education 76*, 1, 28–32.

Nesbitt, E. (2001) 'Religious nurture and young people's spirituality.' In J. Erricker, C. Ota and C. Erricker (eds) *Spiritual Education. Cultural, Religious and Social Differences, New Perspectives for the 21st Century.* Brighton, UK: Sussex Academic.

Newberg, A., d'Aquili, E. and Rause, V. (2001) *Why God Won't Go Away. Brain Science and the Biology of Belief.* New York: Ballantine.

Newby, M. (1996) 'Spiritual development and love of the world.' *International Journal of Children's Spirituality 1*, 1, 44–51.

Noone, R. and Holman, D. (1972) *In Search of the Dream People.* New York: William Morrow.

Nye, R. (1996) 'Childhood spirituality and contemporary developmental psychology.' In R. Best (ed.) *Education, Spirituality and the Whole Child.* London: Cassell.

Ofsted (2004) *Promoting and evaluating pupils' spiritual, moral, social and cultural development.* London: Ofsted.

O'Murchu, D. (1997) *Reclaiming Spirituality. A New Spiritual Framework for Today's World.* Dublin: Gateway.

Oxfam GB (2006a) *Education for Global Citizenship. A Guide for Schools.* Oxford: Oxfam.

Oxfam GB (2006b) *Teaching Controversial Issues.* Oxford: Oxfam.

Persinger, M. (1996) 'Feelings of past lives as expected perturbations within the neurocognitive processes that generate the sense of self: contributions from limbic lability and vectoral hemisphericity.' *Perception and Motor Skills 83*, 3, 1107–1121.

Pridmore, P. and Pridmore, J. (2004) 'Promoting the spiritual development of sick children.' *International Journal of Children's Spirituality 9*, 1, 21–38.

Priestley, J. (2001) 'The experience of religious varieties, William James and the Postmodern Age.' In J. Erricker, C. Ota and C. Erricker (eds) *Spiritual Education. Cultural, Religious and Social Differences, New Perspectives for the 21st Century.* Brighton, UK: Sussex Academic.

Punamäki, R. (1999) 'The role of culture, violence, and personal factors affecting dream content.' *Journal of Cross-cultural Psychology 29*, 2, 320–342.

Ramachandran, V. and Blakeslee, S. (1998) *Phantoms in the Brain.* London: Fourth Estate.

Ranson, D. (2002) *Across the Great Divide Bridging Spirituality and Religion Today.* Strathfield, NSW: St. Paul's.

Resnick, J., Stickgold, R., Rittenhouse, C. and Hobson, A.J. (1994) 'Self-representation and bizarreness in children's dream reports collected in the home setting.' *Consciousness and Cognition 3*, 1, 30–45.

Robinson, E. (1977) *The Original Vision. A Study of the Religious Experience of Childhood.* Oxford: The Religious Experience Unit.

Rogers, G. and Hill, D. (2002) 'Initial primary teacher education students and spirituality.' *International Journal of Children's Spirituality 7*, 3, 273–289.

Rossiter, G. (2005) 'From St Ignatius to Obi Wan Kenobi: An evaluative perspective on spirituality for school education.' *Journal of Religious Education 53*, 1, 3–22.

Roux, C. (2006) 'Children's spirituality in social context: a South African example.' *International Journal of Children's Spirituality 11*, 1, 151–163.

Ruxton, S. (ed.) (2004) *Gender Equality and Men: Learning from Practice.* London, Oxfam GB.

Save the Children (undated). Accessed 24/09/07 at http://www.savethechildren.org.uk/scuk/jsp/resources/details.jsp?id=4620andgroup=resourcesandsection=educationandsubsection=detailsandpagelang=en.

Sandford, T., Hubert, M., Bajos, N. and Bos, H. (1998) 'Sexual behaviour and HIV risk.' In M. Hubert, N. Bajos and T. Sandfort (eds) *Sexual Behaviours and HIV/AIDS in Europe.* London: UCL Press.

Scott, D. (2004) 'Retrospective spiritual narratives: exploring recalled childhood and adolescent spiritual experiences.' *International Journal of Children's Spirituality 9*, 1, 67–79.

Scott, D. (2006). 'Spirituality and identity within/without religion.' In M. de Souza, K. Engebretson, G. Durka, R. Jackson and A. McGrady (eds) *International Handbook of the Religious, Moral and Spiritual Dimensions in Education.* AA Dordrecht, The Netherlands: Springer.

Siegel, A. and Bulkeley, K. (1998) *Dreamcatching: Every Parent's Guide to Exploring and Understanding Children's Dreams and Nightmares.* New York: Three Rivers Press.

Sinetar, M. (2000) *Spiritual Intelligence. What we can Learn from the Early Awakening Child.* New York: Orbis.

Solms, M. (1999) 'The interpretation of dreams and the neurosciences,' presented at the Scientific Meeting of the British Psychoanalytic Society.

Soo Hoo, S. (1993) 'Students as partners in research and restructuring schools.' *The Educational Forum 57*, 386–393.

Sperber, D. (1994) 'The modularity of thought and the epidemiology of representations.' In L. Hirschfeld and S. Gelman (eds) *Mapping the Mind Domain Specificity in Cognition and Culture.* Cambridge: Cambridge University Press.

Stewart, K.R. (1951) 'Dream theory in Malaya.' *Complex 6*, 21–33.

Strauch, I. and Lederbogen, S. (1999) 'The home dreams and waking fantasies of boys and girls ages 9–15: A longitudinal study.' *Dreaming 9*, 2/3, 153–161.

Tacey, D. (1995) *Edge of the Sacred. Transformation in Australia.* Sydney: HarperCollins.

Tacey, D. (2000) *ReEnchantement, the New Australian Spirituality.* Sydney: HarperCollins.

Tacey, D. (2003) *The Spirituality Revolution. The Emergence of Contemporary Spirituality.* Sydney: HarperCollins.

Thatcher, A. (1996) 'Policing the sublime: A wholly (holy?) ironic approach to the spiritual development of children.' In J. Astley and L. Francis (eds) *Christian Theology and Religious Education, Connections and Contradictions.* London: SPCK.

Thatcher, A. (1999) 'Theology, spirituality and the curriculum: An overview.' In A. Thatcher (ed.) *Spirituality and the Curriculum.* London: Cassell.

Thatcher, A. (ed.) (1999) *Spirituality and the Curriculum*. London: Cassell.

Tutu, D. (1995) *An African Prayer Book*. London: Hodder and Stoughton.

UNAIDS (2004) *2004 Report on the Global AIDS Epidemic: Fourth Global Report*. Geneva, Switzerland: UNAIDS.

UNICEF (2002) *The State of the World's Children 2003*. New York: UNICEF.

United Nations (1989) *Convention on the Rights of the Child adopted by the General Assembly of the United Nations on 20 November 1989*. London: HMSO.

Van de Castle, R. (1994) *Our Dreaming Mind*. New York: Random House.

Voiels, V. (1996) 'The inner self and becoming a teacher.' In M. Steiner (ed.) *Developing the Global Teacher: Theory and Practice in Initial Teacher Education*. Stoke-on-Trent: Trentham Books.

Watson, B. (1993) *The Effective Teaching of Religious Education*. London: Longman.

Watson, J. (2003) 'Preparing spirituality for citizenship.' *International Journal of Children's Spirituality* 8, 1, 9–24.

Weller, P (ed.) (1997) *Religions in the UK: A Multi-faith Directory*, Derby: University of Derby and the Interfaith Network for the United Kingdom.

Wellings, K., Wadsworth, J., Johnson, A., Field, J., Whitaker, L and Field, B. (1995) 'Provision of sex education and early sexual experience: the relation examined.' *British Medical Journal* 311, 417–20.

Westerman, W. (2001) 'Youth and adulthood in children's and adults' perspectives.' In J. Erricker, C. Ota and C. Erricker (eds) *Spiritual Education: Cultural, Religious and Social Differences*. Brighton, UK: Sussex Academic Press.

Wilber, K. (2000) 'Waves, streams, states and self: Further considerations for an integral theory of consciousness.' In J. Anderson and R. Forman (eds) *Cognitive Experience*. Thorverton, UK: Imprint Academic.

Wood, E. (2003) 'The power of pupils' perspectives in evidence-based practice: the case of gender underachievement.' *Research Papers in Education* 18, 4, 360–372.

Woolley, R. (2006) 'Education for global citizenship: Developing student teachers' perceptions and practice.' Paper presented at seventh International Conference on Children's Spirituality, University of Winchester, July 2006.

Woolley, R. (2007) 'What makes men...? Masculinity, violence and identity.' In C. Harber, and J. Serf (eds) *Comparative Education and Global Learning*. Birmingham: TIDE Global Learning.

Wright, A. (1996) 'The child in relationship: Towards a communal model of spirituality.' In R. Best (ed.) *Education, Spirituality and the Whole Child*. London: Cassell.

Wright, A. (2000) *Spirituality and Education*. London: Routledge Falmer.

Zohar, D. and Marshall, I. (2000) *SQ Spiritual Intelligence, the Ultimate Intelligence*. London: Bloomsbury.

Subject Index

Author Index